DATE DUE

Demco, Inc. 38-293

JAN 3 1 2006

Diversions &
Animadversions

Diversions &
Animadversions

Essays from *The New Criterion*

Alexander Coleman
Roger Kimball, editor

With a preface by the editor
and an introduction by Denis Donoghue

Transaction Publishers
New Brunswick (U.S.A.) and London (U.K.)

This book is printed on acid-free paper that meets the American National
Standard for Permanence of Paper for Printed Library Materials.

Library of Congress Catalog Number: 2005051445
ISBN: 0-7658-0305-4
Printed in the United States of America

Library of Congress Cataloging-in-Publication Data

Coleman, Alexander.
    Diversions and animadversions : essays from The New criterion /
    Alexander Coleman ; edited and with a preface by Roger Kimball ;
    introduction by Denis Donoghue.
        p. cm.
    ISBN 0-7658-0305-4 (acid-free paper)
    1. Music—20th century—History and criticism. I. Kimball, Roger,
    1953- II. Title.

ML60.C65 2005
780'.9—dc22   2005051445

Contents

Preface   *vii*

Introduction   *xi*

Part One

Eça de Quierós   5

The Gypsy Balladeer   27

Fantastic Argentine   33

Part Two

The Sibelius Question   49

Berg's Femmes Fatales   65

"Dallas" auf Deutsch   74

"Der Rosenkavalier"   87

Toscanini in His Letters   103

Houses of Repute   110

Authentically Bland   123
Orpheus in Hell   132
At Last, the Promised Land?   146
The Virgilian Agenda   155
Sviatoslav Richter, 1915–1997   167
City Opera; Stuyvesant Park   174
Alicia de Larrocha at Carnegie Hall   184

Part Three

Life in Basqueland   195
¿O Plomo o Plata?   205
Letter from Vienna   218

Preface

by Roger Kimball

THIS VOLUME contains nearly all of the criticism that John Alexander Coleman wrote for *The New Criterion*. His first essay, about the Argentinian writer Adolfo Bioy Casares, appeared in October 1994; his last piece—a review of a new translation of poems by Federico García Lorca—appeared eight years later in October 2002. By that time, John was already ill with the cancer that killed him in June 2003 at the age of 67. The essays are reprinted without alteration, except for the silent correction of a handful of typographical errors.

I met John in the early 1990s at a monthly seminar on modernism sponsored jointly by *The New Criterion* and New York University, where John taught Spanish and Portuguese literature from "forever" (as he said) until his (early and eagerly sought) retirement in 1997. From the start, it was clear that John was a man of rare wit, capacious learning, and eager if gently ironical curiosity. At those seminars, John displayed his easy mastery of literature—not just Spanish and Latin American literature, but the entire modernist tradition. He was an expert in Borges (whose work he translated, edited, and expounded), and had a deep grasp of Eliot, Henry James, Stevens, Santayana, and many other figures. But it soon became clear that John's greatest passion was for music. He had an impressive command of the classical repertory, and, I know from have spent many hours at his house in Wilton, Connecticut, an equally impressive command of jazz. Indeed, John did not discriminate among genres: only between good music and bad, the excellent and the false, sentimental, or poorly executed.

John published on a wide variety of subjects literary and musical for numerous scholarly journals as well as for *The New York Times Book Review*, *The New York Review of Books*, and other literary journals. For *The New Criterion*, he wrote delightfully erudite pieces on such neglected figures as the Portuguese novelist and man of letters Eça de Queirós, an abundance of music criticism, and incisive reports on the cultural situation in the (invariably balmy) places his inveterate travels took him.

IN HIS INTRODUCTION to this book, John's old friend Denis Donoghue clears up the mystery of why the person I have been referring to as "John Coleman" wrote under the by-line "Alexander Coleman." I am grateful to Mr. Donoghue for his illuminating and affectionate introduction. I am also grateful to Irving Louis Horowitz, *genius loci* of Transaction Publishers, for agreeing to publish this volume, to Alexandra

Kimball for editorial help, and to the staff of *The New Criterion*, especially to David Spelber, for help in preparing this volume. John Coleman was as good a friend as Alexander Coleman was an astute and wide-ranging critical observer. We miss his ebullient presence in the pages of *The New Criterion* and, even more, his friends miss it in their lives. I am delighted to be able to make this portion of John's work available between hardcovers.

August 2004

Introduction
by Denis Donoghue

HIS FULL NAME was John Alexander Coleman. I once asked him why he wrote under the name "Alexander Coleman," and he said that he did not want to collide with John Coleman, a journalist and critic he admired who wrote for various magazines in London. J.A.C.'s friends who spoke to him in Spanish called him Juano, so far as I could judge. He called most of us "Doctor," the ladies in the company "Madame," and a few of us "Maestro."

I met him for the first time in Cambridge, Massachusetts, when I was teaching at the Harvard Summer School. In addition to teaching, I was trying to write a book on modern American poetry, a project I could not even get started on that summer till John said "talk it to me and I'll type it as you go." So I started on Whitman. By the end of the summer John had supplied me with an encouraging body of typescript. He had learnt to type at some American army base, doing secretarial work as an alternative to going to war. His skill with the typewriter partly explains why he was never irritated by the necessity of writing a second or a third draft of an essay or a review. He was one of the last of us to buy a PC; he could not see the point of it or how helpful it could be in revising one's work. But when he retired from teaching and bought a computer, he used it to read Latin American newspapers and journals for two or three hours every morning.

That summer in Cambridge, John educated me in his kinds of jazz. One evening he insisted that we go down to Boston to hear Ben Webster, who was playing in a basement club. John was on cordial terms with Webster and introduced me to him. To acknowledge my being an Irishman, the great man played "Danny Boy," despite the fact that someone at the back of the room, far gone in drink, kept shouting "Give us 'Trees.'" John's taste in jazz suited me well: we shared Dave Brubeck, Stan Getz, Ellis Larkin, Goodman, Ellington, and Jack Teagarten. We did not quarrel about John Coltrane, whom John couldn't abide. He agreed with Philip Larkin, too, in having no time for Charlie Parker.

John and I were already friends when I came to teach in the English Department at New York University. He was professor in the Department of Spanish and Portuguese, after a short and mostly unhappy stint at Wellesley College. He was a splendid teacher, vivid in the service of Latin American literature. He also taught a course on Literature and Music. But he had limitations. He had no interest in theoretical

issues, which during those years were nearly ines-
capable. He taught his favorite authors without
spending a moment on the ideological questions that
supposedly took precedence. Nor did he show the
least interest in my little efforts in the direction of
Theory. His attitude was: "This too will pass."

I tried to discuss with him the niceties of Adorno's
Philosophy of Modern Music, a book in which
Adorno adjudicates between Stravinsky and Schoenberg, much to Schoenberg's advantage. I had read the
book in the library of Trinity College, Dublin before
buying a copy for slow study. But I could not bring
John into the debate. He liked many of Stravinsky's
works and a few of Schoenberg's: he saw no point in
driving their differences into a dispute. In the present
book Coleman refers, justly indeed, to the critical arguments about Sibelius, but he is happy to leave them
unresolved. He had little interest in conclusions. I
once urged him to write a book called *Aspiring to
Music,* taking its point of departure from Walter
Pater's claim that all the arts "constantly aspire
toward the condition of music." Start with Schopen-
hauer, I said, then take on Nietzsche and Wagner, and
bring the book to a grand end with Schoenberg and
Thomas Mann in *Doctor Faustus.* Add Berg and
Webern for good measure. John nodded his approval
and changed the subject. I could see that the project
was too argumentative for his liking. He was not out
for anyone's blood.

What he mainly wanted to do was to listen to
music in congenial company. The eccentric house he

built for himself in Wilton, Connecticut was ideal for the purpose: it was designed for conviviality as much as for shelter. John was fortunate in his companions there. Next door he had the folk-singer Bill Crofut and his wife, the painter Susie Crofut. The Brubecks lived a mile or two down the road. The poet and translator Alastair Reid was in New York City. David Hall, master-discographer, was in frequent communication. Fred Binkley, who lived in New York City, knew even more jazz than John did. Robert Penn Warren and his wife Eleanor Clark were a few hours north from Wilton. "A scene well set and excellent company," as Yeats has it. Between one warmhearted occasion and the next, John had his record collection, vast but not omnivorous: he trusted his taste. As a member of the Wilton Library music committee, he kept himself up to date, nudged forward by David Shuster, John's colleague and mine at NYU and himself an accomplished pianist. There were always new things to hear, and old things in different interpretations. I must have heard Bernstein's recording of the "Enigma Variations" ten times over the years in Wilton: Mahler's Ninth under Bruno Walter, Lipatti's final concert in Besançon, nearly anything conducted by Haitink, anything by Benny Goodman, Ellington, Webster. The evening had to conclude with Pavarotti singing "Nessun Dorma" and Teagarten playing "Lover."

Evenings in New York were more carefully ordained. We must see a play or two; *Butley* and, for a reason I never understood, *The Common Pursuit*.

Mostly it was music; a dress rehearsal by Bernstein, Richard Stoltzman playing Mozart's Clarinet Concerto, Christa Ludwig singing *Das Lied von der Erde*. We often heard Alberta Hunter at the Cookery (now long gone), and more pianists than I can name at the Cedar Tavern. One night we trekked far uptown to hear Dick Welstead, but I didn't warm to the occasion. Stride piano doesn't appeal to me: too many notes.

When John started writing for *The New Criterion* he became even more assiduous, doing his homework, reading all the books, comparing interpretations. I was with him on one of the evenings of the Sibelius festival he writes about in the present book, when we heard the Lahti Symphony Orchestra conducted by Osmo Vänskä. John had heard the Lahti before, on a trip to Helsinski, and had no qualms in preferring it to the London Symphony Orchestra under Sir Colin Davis.

Although John was a gifted teacher of Latin American literature, he was timid in writing about literature itself. His book on Eça de Queirós is well thought of in the profession, but John had little inclination to follow one good book by writing another. He found literary writing arduous, despite his prowess on the typewriter. In a hundred evenings we rarely discussed a poem or a novel. He wanted to hear more music and then to talk about it: about music and the lore of music, the people who made it available, composers, instrumentalists, singers, conductors.

So far as I know, he had little formal education in

music. He took possession of music by listening to it and by being intelligent in experiencing it. He had listened to more music than anyone else in my vicinity, leaving aside the few professional musicians I have known. He admired the scholars of music, especially those who intuited—without claiming to understand—the impingement of life and art. A case in point: Ernest Newman on Wagner. But he had no ambition to write technically about music. I doubt that he ever looked at *The Music Quarterly* or read an essay by Susan McClary. He relied on his ear, the mind's ear, and his sense of music—opera especially—as a social art, even though most of us get our music by radio and the CD rather than by going to Lincoln Center. The critics he admired were intense amateurs, unprofessional minds at large: B. H. Haggin on music, Robert Garis on ballet.

So it is surprising that John Coleman's writing for *The New Criterion* included mood pieces, evocations of place, cities of sounds, as well as social and political commentary. It still surprises me that he wrote so spiritedly about Bilbao and Basque Nationalism, and about the Mexican economy and the student strikes. We didn't talk much about politics. His father, mayor of Hartford for many years, brought John, as a child, to FDR's funeral in Washington, D.C. So far as I know, John remained a Democrat all his life. He and I attended a wake for JFK in Philadelphia, summoned by a woman who claimed to have been one of the President's lovers. "Greensleeves," supposedly Kennedy's favorite piece of music, was played throughout the evening. But John and I rarely discussed political issues. We never argued about "the ongoing debasement of our culture," to which he refers in this book, or the fact, as I suppose it is a fact, that "anything goes these days." We talked of the bizarre Wagner family and what one was to make of Virgil Thomson. But even on such issues, John showed no urge to be definitive. He was primarily an essayist in appreciation. Posterity would decide—and time enough, too. Reading these essays again, I hear the voice I knew and cared for, a voice deliberative but not doctrinal. And every now and again, as in the essay on Schoenberg's *Moses und Aron*, I hear a sharper voice, a more telling articulation, which I'm afraid I was not acute enough to attend to at the time.

Diversions and Animadversions

Part One

Eça de Queirós

THERE IS a photograph of the Portuguese novelist José Maria Eça de Queirós (1845–1900) surrounded by his friends in a Lisbon salon in the late 1880s. They all convey a notable elegance of attire and toilette—striped pants, burnished top hats, abundant beards, and finely waxed upturned moustaches. Eça de Queirós is seated at a table in front of the group, walking stick in hand, eyes cast down demurely. This group of eleven men represented the intellectual elite of Portugal at that time. They were poets, diplomats, statesmen, politicians who for a time gathered weekly at the Hotel Braganza or at the home of one of the group.

Energetic achievers in many realms, they paradoxically called themselves *Os vencidos da vida* ("Those defeated by life"). The morose title given to the group has as much to do with the apparent glories of Portugal's past—the adventures in Brazil, Africa, and India—as with the tedium and political paralysis which reigned in Portugal throughout the nineteenth century (and from which it has hardly escaped in the twentieth). *Os vencidos* were both children of an exhausted romanticism and freshly minted students of Marx and Proudhon. As such, they had critical insights into the decadence of Portugal and were ready with remedies that would bring about a long-awaited spiritual and political salvation.

But as intellectuals who absorbed the French critical spirit wholesale, in both its eighteenth- and nineteenth-century formulations, they were dogged by a pessimism about what really might be done with the country once their generation came to power. They did come to power, and nothing really changed. Their idealism foundered on the torpor of traditional Portugal. Eça's perverse explanation of the meaning behind the label *Os vencidos da vida* is worthy of note:

> If a young man has as his supreme ideal in life the career of hairdresser, and he attains that station, he is a conqueror, a great conqueror of life. If, on the other hand, a young man of twenty wants to be a millionaire, a sublime poet, or an undefeated general, and after the most strenuous effort reaches only halfway toward the vaunted million, the poem, or the full regalia of a general, then he is to all effects someone who is defeated in life, a dead man alive, all dressed up for burial with his frock coat and top hat concealing the luster of resignation before life.

This is pure Eça de Queirós—boundless energies expended in a critical attack against old, Catholic Portugal while being consciously aware of the futility of the enterprise. As for his readership, the census taken in the year of Eça's death tallied only 21 percent of the populace as at all literate; he knew from the start that Portugal moves only belatedly, and sometimes takes a step or two back in time at that.

Eça's achievement as a writer is imposing by any measure. A recent edition of his complete works in Portuguese—in painfully small print—makes up over five thousand pages of stories, novellas, novels, literary and political essays, a book about traveling through Egypt on the occasion of the opening of the Suez Canal, hundreds of letters, even an inexplicable translation of H. Rider Haggard's *King Solomon's Mines*. Eça's major novels gradually found their way into English in the 1950s and 1960s. The retentive reader now "getting on in years" may vaguely recall the titles of those translations, now mostly out of print—*The Sin of Father Amaro*, *Cousin Bazilio*, *The Mandarin*, *The Relic*, *The Maias*, *The Illustrious House of Ramires*, *The City and the Mountains*—along with the attendant prologues and enthusiastic reception by such critics as Francis Steegmuller and Stanley Edgar Hyman. Just recently, New Directions published a new translation of a lurid novella by Eça under the title *The Yellow Sofa*, and has also reissued Eça's masterpiece *The Illustrious House of Ramires* with a preface by V. S. Pritchett. There is also an edition of the fantasy novel *The Relic* available from the Dedalus Press. At this juncture, all the rest of his fiction and work in other genres, such as the delicious *Letters from England*, has long gone out of print.

I bring up the existence of my own study of his novels, *Eça de Queirós and European Realism* (New York University Press, 1980) only to dramatize how much fury and rage the personality and work of this author can still awaken in a particular ideological and religious sector of Portuguese readership. Just after the publication of my book, a grand dame of Lisbon expressed to me her displeasure upon hearing that Eça's work was beginning to have at least a fitful readership in the United States. "That dreadful man," she intoned, "did irreparable damage to Portugal, and he will never be forgiven." This is the same writer that Emile Zola characterized as "greater than my own dear master Flaubert." To some Portuguese of a certain cast of mind, Eça still remains merely the provocateur, the monocled dandy, the enemy of old beliefs and settled custom.

His critical invective against Portugal—against the mythification of ancient glories, for instance—and his debunking of the prowess of its adventurers, dis-coverers, and colonizers, were "barbs," as he called them, designed to shock the nation into a realization of what were the true effects of Portugal's colonial activities. Like Spain in its relation to its "colonies" in the Americas, Portugal in his view came to be a sup-plicant in relation to Brazil:

> We [Portuguese] were in that dreary position towards them of an old aristocrat, a broken old bachelor, toothless and tottering, who trembles and dribbles before a buxom comely housekeeper. It was we who

were really the colony: and it was with a fearfully beating heart, between a *Salve Regina* and a *Laus perenne*, that we held out our hands there for alms.

In his early years and well into maturity, Eça was the incarnation of resentment against Portuguese society as he found it. He had his reasons.

When pressed about his childhood, early years and adolescence, he would dismiss the topic from any inquiry or conversation. As he curtly declared to a friend, "Facts for my biography—I don't know how to provide any. I am just like the Republic of Andorra—I don't have a history." The melodrama of the circumstances of his birth and formative years explains why he took such pains to remain silent.

José Maria Eça de Queirós was born in 1845 of unmarried parents. His father was a local judge just out of law school, the mother barely nineteen. On the baptismal certificate, she is listed as "mother unknown." Seven days before she gave birth, Eça's father sent a gelid letter addressed simply to "Madame" ("Senhora"), assuring her that the child would be removed from her sight and educated by him. Because of his lower station in society—her family was of middling aristocratic lineage close to the monarchy—she refused to marry the miscreant until her mother, on her deathbed, finally extracted the daughter's reluctant assent to marry the man. The ceremony took place in 1849, four years after the birth of the child. Although the now legitimate couple in due course had six more children, the infant "born before time" was not permitted to live with the family—those he had every right to think of as father, mother, brothers, and sisters—until he had graduated from the University of Coimbra some twenty-one years later. Moreover, Eça's parents did not formally recognize him until producing a dry document for legal purposes just before Eça's own marriage *forty-one* years after his birth, in 1886, a ceremony neither parent chose to attend.

Eça was essentially an orphan, first cared for by a wet nurse, then handed over to the paternal grandparents, then off to boarding school, then university. Vacations were spent with an aunt. In all his five thousand pages of texts, mothers or fathers are rarely present. Eça was the rejected child, the *enjeitadinho*. Most of the protagonists in his novels are either orphans or cared for by proxy authority figures. Needless to say, Freudian critics have pondered heavily over the relation of his early childhood to the kind of retributive literature he was to produce over the years.

As an undergraduate at the hallowed University of Coimbra, he was both an avid amateur actor and distant participant in student uprisings. Eça remembered those extracurricular activities much later: "In four years we instigated three student revolutions with all the classic elements in place: manifestoes to the populace, rock throwing and street uproars, a rusty pistol underneath every cape, fiery effigies of rectors burning away as we executed jungle dances around the pyre." With law degree in hand, he tried out a career as journalist in the provinces and as quondam lawyer, but these attempts each lasted for only a few months. Out of the blue (but probably due to his father's machinations), an invitation was received by "Monsieur le Chevalier de Queirós" to attend the opening of the Suez Canal. He left Lisbon in October 1869, in the company of a good friend, Count Luís Resende, who became his brother-in-law seventeen years later when Eça married Emília de Resende.

IF EÇA'S JOURNALISM and occasional writings before the Egyptian trip are a mélange of conflicting allegiances, ranging from fiery social revolutionary to dour Proudhonian moralist, another Eça magically appeared in Cairo:

> I confess that in the Turkish baths, under the magnetic pressure of the masseur, listening to the water dripping in the hookah, I decided that all vices and all crimes were natural, rational, and legitimate! I wanted to be a caliph, I wanted to sleep on divans of satin, enveloped in the aroma of aloes and the perfume of roses . . . . I would eat delicious, spicy things, I would order that the stomachs of my slaves be cut open in order to examine the disposition of their entrails, I would cut off the heads of Abyssinian women in order to feel the warm blood of those hot-tempered women of the Nile, I would drape pearls over my hounds, I would forget my people, and I would order that all bodies that were not divinely beautiful be tossed into the Nile!
>
> Happily my jacket made in Nottingham, England

was hanging right there as a presence of reality, as a wholesome memento.

After leaving Cairo, Eça and Count Resende visited the pyramids of Giza and the temples and ruins of Memphis. After attending the inauguration of the canal, they went on to Palestine, Syria, and Lebanon, returning to Lisbon on January 3, 1870.

Upon his return, Eça found his friends in a state of high intellectual ferment. They were organizing a series of public lectures, which would expose the deteriorated state of Portuguese society and culture and offer prescriptions for a spiritual renewal. One participant took on the subject of "The Causes of the Decadence of the Iberian People," another gave a critical overview of the present state of Portuguese literature. Eça chose to be the standard bearer of "Realism as an Expression of New Art." Almost as a sartorial defense against this championing of Flaubert, Zola, and Courbet, Eça appeared before the public dressed as an elegant diplomat ready to present his credentials at the Court of Saint James: "Irreproachable buttoned-up frock coat, high collar, white vest, satin tie, glossy shoes, gray gloves," according to one observer. The arguments in the lecture, on the other hand, were primitive. According to Eça, realism should be a literature proceeding from experience through physiology, "the science of temperaments and inner character." In his glosses of Flaubert, Eça saw the new literary science only as an instrument for *o artista vingador* ("the vengeful artist"), the denunciatory moralist exposing the vulgarities and pretensions of the new democratic age. The lecture got many things wrong from the point of view of critical accuracy, but it was more than enough of a platform for him to launch his first major novel, *The Sin of Father Amaro*, in its three successive versions: 1875, 1876, and the definitive amplification of 1880.

Eighteen-seventy-one was Eça's last year resident in his own country. After entering the foreign service of Portugal, he was posted first to Cuba (1872–1874), then on to Newcastle-on-Tyne, remaining immensely productive in what he considered to be inhospitable circumstances. He then was sent to Bristol in 1878 (only marginally more pleasant), and finally held the esteemed ranking of Portuguese consul in Paris from 1888 until 1900, the year of his death, probably of a repeatedly undiagnosed amoebic dysentery.

Accompanying the insistent Freudianism of Eça's critics, much has been made of his exile after 1872, and even more has been made of his marriage to Emília de Resende in 1886. At just over forty years of age, Eça de Queirós married a woman of twenty-eight who was his polar opposite—she was relatively uneducated, a severely conservative Catholic, pious and God-fearing in the extreme, just as he was the representative of Voltairean sarcasm and irreverence toward the phenomenon of belief in general. As he described himself around this time, "I am the carcass of an old cynic." His letters to his friends, and even to his future brother-in-law, point to a *mariage de raison*. After all, four of her sisters had already entered the convent, and she had just been abruptly jilted by another member of Os vencidos, Luís de Soveral.

Until their respective dying days, Eça de Queirós's four children furiously denied any kind of cynical arrangement or emotional compromise in their parents' sentimental relations, and swore to their father's undying love for their mother. Nonetheless, a perusal of the complete correspondence between husband and wife, including his gruesome final letters from Southern France and Switzerland where he went in a futile search for a cure, points to a willful determination on his part to create a home and a family anyway, anyhow, and to feign and disguise the inner self in order to attain these things—the ambiance that was so assiduously denied him in his childhood.

What also was consistently denied him and his family was any degree of financial security. Eça was an extravagant spender, it is true, but he was ill-paid even as consul in Paris and was the victim of high piracy on the part of his Lisbon publishers. He never came anywhere near to getting out from under monstrous debts. Even the last letters to his wife continually harp on the need for household economies. She, in turn, seems always to be without a sou in their Neuilly home. In any case, at the time none of the four children had any idea that their father was a writer, an artist. They were thrilled with his being a consul, and that was that. Until her death in 1934, the widow assiduously celebrated his memory, but at the same time she did everything in her power to prevent the publication of texts she considered indecent. When, in 1922, Valéry Larbaud asked for permission to have Eça's most scabrous and irreverent novel, *The Relic*, translated into French, permission was denied. Indeed, one study of incest between mother and son, *A Tragédia da Rua das Flores*, remained in manuscript and was not published until 1980; such was the censorious legacy of Emília de Resende.

EÇA'S PERMANENT exile from Portugal, in spite of lengthy consular leaves, produced a crisis in the formative principles of his literature, a crisis which at the same time was a catalyst to write another kind of literature not so slavishly dependent upon what he finally got to think of as realist dogma. As always, he is his own best critic:

> I cannot depict Portugal in Newcastle. In order to write any page, any line, I have to make two violent efforts: disengage myself entirely from the impression which I get from the society around me and then evoke, by means of a tension of reminiscence, the society which is far away. This makes my characters less and less Portuguese, but they are not more English because of this; they are beginning to be conventional . . . either I go back to the environment in which I can produce, by the experimental method— that is, return to Portugal—or I will have to surrender to a purely fantastical and humorous literature.

As an early admiring student of Flaubertian

meticulousness, Eça in his first two novels gives us a baleful vision of provincial Portuguese society. This is the background busily laid out in *The Sin of Father Amaro* with its rich cast of gossips, useless functionaries, and aged but still lusty spinsters all under the thrall of gourmand clerics with easy sexual mores. Here, eros is the anarchic force, the shatterer of propriety. The fervent parishioner Amélia is seduced by the young Father Amaro just out of the seminary. After she gives birth, the infant is taken away by the crazed priest and drowned (in the first two versions) or handed over to a sinister female custodian, "the weaver of angels," who disposes of the infant by neglect within a month (final version). In his second novel, *Cousin Bazilio*, the happily married but bored Luiza—modelled distantly on Emma Bovary but drawn with more compassion than the implacable Flaubert's heroine—dies of a mysterious malady after her frivolous seduction by the interloper Cousin Bazilio. As sympathetic observer and moral monitor, Eça brings Luiza's predicaments and quandaries to life, all while having her as-yet-unknowing husband, Jorge, say some terrible things about the fate of any adulteress, without, of course, having his wife in mind:

> "If the husband is deceived, I'm for death. I don't care if it's in an abyss, a room, or the street—she must be killed. Kill her at once!" They all protested at this outburst of Jorge's, calling him a "wild beast," "Othello," "Bluebeard," and so on. Jorge only

laughed, peacefully filling his pipe. Luiza sat crocheting in silence.

In early Eça, eros is indecorous at the very least, often illegitimate by nature, and vertiginously suicidal at the very worst. Venus was a perilous goddess for Eça—he called her *Venus Tenebrosa*, or "Sinister Venus." Between desire and the social order, society does prevail, and the adulterer of any sex is hounded out, if not eliminated. As for the child born out of wedlock, it must be cast aside, if not worse. His writings from around this time, aside from their rich orchestration of provincial inanities, revolve around the games of love and marriage, the consequences of the passionate life. After all, Eça himself was a "born" expert in all these matters—too much eros, too little agapē.

IF ALL THE FOREGOING gives the impression of an author who began his career on a path of unremitting grimness under the sway of French realism and naturalism, things do lighten up considerably, although the tragic sense is never lost. The problems of being a writer in exile were indeed taxing, but Eça's reading of Dickens, George Eliot, and Thackeray during the English years had a soothing effect. They broadened his vision and softened what might be thought of as the novelistic preaching of the early years. Furthermore, there was a growing disenchantment with France. As he fulfilled his long-cherished dream of permanent residency in Paris, he began to sever the spiritual bond that had sustained him throughout his student years as fledgling literary theoretician and as a writer renowned for being the foremost exponent of realism in the Portuguese language.

Not exactly a volte-face, this was part of the ongoing process of self-criticism which was his own tortured way of making literature. Self-doubt was a paradoxically driving force in him. At times he diminished himself—these critical flagellations were always administered to his own writing after a particularly distinguished work was finished. For instance, having just published the taut *Cousin Bazilio*, Eça brings up the glaring distance he senses between what he has just achieved and the French masters. No one seems able to tell him that this is hardly the point:

> By the way, what did you think of *Cousin Bazilio*? Idiotic, don't you think? "Ce n'est pas ça. Ce n'est pas ça du tout." The style is limpid, it has energy, transparence, precision, "netteté." But there is no life in it. It lacks "vigor" (poigne). The characters—you will see—do not have the sense of life that we have; they are not exactly "des images découpées," but they have a gelatinous musculature. . . . I construct cardboard worlds . . . some little thing is missing within, the small cerebral vibration; I am an irremissible imbecile.

Perhaps mechanisms to elicit contrary praise from friends, these exercises by this literary anchorite could fill a very peculiar anthology; they all point to a *via negativa* in his own processes, goads to do better or simply something else.

The two fantasy novels of the 1880s—*The Mandarin* and *The Relic*—are to many his supreme achievements. The new direction is indicated in the prologue (written in French) to a translation of *The Mandarin*, where the latest version of Eça as writer has a bracing dialogue with the Eça of old. The new writer breezily dismisses the tenets of realism—"We tried to put in our works much observation, much 'humanity'; but in studying our neighbors, small rentiers, or petty employees, it turned out that we soon regretted those times when it was permissible, without being old-fashioned, to celebrate handsome knights in shining armor." The Portuguese artist has suffered too long, he says, in an atmosphere of reality, modernity, and banality. He asks for temporary license to unfetter the imagination, "where one no longer accepts the inconvenient submission to truth, to the torture of analysis, to the impertinent tyranny of reality."

While *The Mandarin* has this prologue of considerable theoretical importance, *The Relic* is by far the better book, if only because of the fact that its insouciance, its celebration of duplicity and hypocrisy marks an imaginative liberation in Eça. It is his most jocose venture into the episodic picaresque genre.

Young Teodorico is a hedonist parasite living as coddled nephew of the aged ultra-Catholic spinster Aunt Titi. She possesses a fortune that he will inherit if he leads a saintly life. Seeing what must be done but being who he is, he begins an orgy of dissimulation—daily mass dressed in black, luncheons with Aunt Titi and a group of malevolent back-biting priests, followed up by evenings spent with a treacherous Spanish prostitute; he is always home by eleven, just in time for the nightly litany.

As the coronation of his duplicity, he promises to take a trip to the Holy Land to bring her back a relic which will guarantee her good health and eternal life in the other world. On the way, another kind of relic is obtained by Teodorico—a nightdress given to him by a golden-haired English beauty, "in remembrance of all our joy." Once in Jerusalem, he visits the Holy Sepulchre in top hat and gloves, obtains something that looks like a crown of thorns, and wraps it in a package identical to the one containing the nightdress. In a drunken dream, he witnesses Christ's condemnation, crucifixion, and resurrection, all while brandishing a very contemporary Cuban cigar. As Eça's character sees Christ's final moments, he is drugged, brought down off the cross, duly placed in the tomb, but dies soon after. The Resurrection is promulgated nonetheless, for "it is necessary that the prophecies be fulfilled."

Back in Lisbon, it is perhaps inevitable that Teodorico presents Aunt Titi not with the promised crown of thorns, but with the sullied nightgown in the identical packaging. With her cries of "Swine" ringing in his ears, he is disinherited, his only regret being that he was incapable of affirming at the crucial moment, without qualms, that the garment was "the nightdress of Saint Mary Magdalene. . . . Who would have doubted such an absurdity?"

As a grand *boutade*, there is nothing like it in all of Eça's work; its boisterous invention and richly organized subversiveness make it also a special literary artifact in European fiction. First brought into print in English by Alfred A. Knopf in 1925, reissued in the Fifties, and again in 1995, this is a novel that begs for reconsideration.

All throughout the 1880s, in a parallel effort accompanying these two works of a "fantastic" nature, Eça was carefully preparing another analysis of and assault on the nature of Portuguese society, its many faults and foibles. This grand novel of some 630-odd pages in the last available English translation is called *The Maias* (1888). A history of the decline of a family over three generations, it is his most carefully elaborated work and the one which reflects his most pressing ambitions toward a historical, political, and societal fidelity to what he saw as the continuing crisis in Portugal in the latter half of the nineteenth century. Again, we can calculate the greatness of the novel by the invective that the author directed against it during a long gestation. For instance, here he is in a letter to a friend dated 1884.

> I am plugging away at *The Maias*, that vast machine of al fresco painting in annoyingly monumental proportions, done with darkish colors, overblown and frivolous, all of which may well earn me the name of the Michelangelo of the insipid. Oh well.

Plot is the least of *The Maias*, following the fortunes of the family from the generation of old Afonso da Maia, an austere and grave gentleman of benevolent and generous spirit, to his son Pedro, a suicide after having been abandoned by a treacherous wife, down to his only grandson, Carlos Eduardo, orphaned at an early age and brought up by Afonso. This appealing yet vague and undirected child will in due course take as his mistress and future wife a woman later discovered to be his sister, long ago abducted by the mother and thought to be dead.

This is the kind of tawdry operatic libretto which Eça adored and loved to work with, since he always fed on the inane and the ludicrous—the materials of melodrama. Against the weight of the plot, Eça paints magnificent scenery of a whole class wasting away its life—an excursion to Sintra, a horserace at the Hippodrome, a scene at the newspaper, a mock duel, a literary soirée at a theater. In the novel, there are no longer any Manichaean commonplaces in the making of the characters but rather a density in human complexity that the author had not achieved before. And, unlike any other novel of Eça, the characters age before our eyes; the erosion of time moves both characters and events toward a fatal conclusion.

Another singular aspect of *The Maias* is the spectacle of Eça inserting himself in his novel as an alter ego named João de Ega. Like Eça, who always used to insist that "Portugal was a country translated from the French into slang," João de Ega, with his "cashmere spats, long hair, and tie with an opal horseshoe pin," will declaim that "Everything is imported in this country: laws, ideas, philosophies, themes, aesthetics, sciences, styles, industries, fashions, manners, jokes. Everything reaches us in packing cases by the mail-boat."

João de Ega is a writer in the long process of producing an epic, "The History of an Atom," which will describe the story of his atoms since the beginning of time: the primeval muck, then to a plant, then to an orangutan, then on to the lips of Plato and Jesus. "It's a Bible," his friends insist.

The incest in *The Maias* is the culmination not only of Eça's dark views about the passions, but also of his picture of the idle upper class of Lisbon working away at its own brand of futilities. As an observer noted, "The incest represents [a] kind of narcissism, the sterility of an elite." It is the summation of a class enclosed within the walls of its egos, their own circles, their own kind. For Eça de Queirós, there was no other Portugal—the illiterate silent peasant was only "landscape."

As noted above, only three works of Eça de Queirós are currently in print. One, *The Illustrious House of Ramires* (New Directions) was published in the year of the author's death without his having gone over the galley proofs with his usual "Benedictine" care. The novel tells of a charming, Mittyish aristocrat, the last remains of a feudal lineage going back to the tenth century, who for therapeutic reasons is in the process of writing a Scott-like historical novel drawing on martial events from the family's history.

As he writes (with many gory samples gleefully furnished by Eça) the protagonist becomes, by means of this parodic pastiche, an artist in life, newly galvanized as practicing politician and colonist in Africa. This is Eça's most mordant and affectionate view of what a "return to old values" signified for him at the end. As always, the heroics of the past dissolve away into comic deflations in the present.

Besides *The Relic*, the only other work now available to us, *The Yellow Sofa*, also under the New Directions imprint, is quite another matter, and deserves some comment. After Eça's death in 1900, a mass of unpublished manuscripts was brought back to Portugal, where it remained for a considerable number of years. Many of these manuscripts were brought to light by Eça's not untalented son, also named José Maria d'Eça de Queirós. These works, such as the one here presented as *The Yellow Sofa*, gradually appeared seriatim in the 1920s. The son was praised for the filial care and scruple which he had so obviously applied to them. It was assumed, no proof to the contrary, that the son had simply deciphered the scrawls and put everything in order. But now that a new critical edition of Eça de Queirós is in process under the general editorship of Professor Carlos Reis of the University of Coimbra, we now discover that the son had authorial ambitions of his own. He was not the modest transmitter of his father's texts, but rather an energetic and highly aggressive editor and author.

In the particular case of *The Yellow Sofa* (known in

Portuguese as *Alves & Cª.*), the new critical edition of this novella demonstrates that the son took it upon himself to improve the text he found in his father's trunk. According to the analysis of Jonathan Keates in his treatment of the matter in the *Times Literary Supplement* (October 17, 1997), "semi-colons and dashes were either changed into commas or else silently removed, the syntax and grammatical structure of sentences were rearranged, and José Maria saw nothing wrong with interpolating additional adjectives in order to intensify the tone at certain points in the story." In another volume of this critical edition, it was found that the son had made some 15,000 alterations to his father's take-off on Balzac's *Lost Illusions*, the work Eça tentatively titled *The Capital!*

So it would seem that all of the son's energetic disinterment of his father's posthumous legacy will have to be scrutinized and cleansed with great scholarly care. In the case of this translated version of Eça's son's edition of *The Yellow Sofa*, the story of a Lisbon businessman cuckolded by his partner at the office who finally takes back his wife and forgives her, the reader can have a considerable degree of confidence in its literary efficacy. As noted above, however, a scrupulous edition of this same work has been issued by the distinguished scholar Professor Luiz Fagundes Duarte, and it is quite different from the son's version. The professor's is more pungent and economical, all retouches removed.

In retrospect, Eça's readers should not have put so much faith in what we now know to be bogus authorship disguised as filial zeal. In any case, it is good to know that fresh versions of the Queirósian canon, posthumous or not, will be available in due course, minus the emendations.

The Nobel Prize for literature was recently awarded to José Saramago, the first writer in the Portuguese language to be so honored. Eça de Queirós could never have been a candidate, for the simple reason that he died the year before the first prizes were announced. But Eça would surely have wryly recognized a brotherhood of critical spirit between himself and Saramago, a political dissident (longtime member of the Communist Party), pointed critic of Portuguese traditionalism, and equally an exile, though in this case a voluntary one in livid protest against the Portuguese government's refusal to offer his works as official candidates for international literary awards. Saramago's novels take up many of the political themes in Eça's work, but they view them with an optic which reminds many readers of the luminous mythification of political realities in the work of Gabrial García Márquez. But Saramago is very much his own vituperative self. In any case, the choice of Saramago, as is often the case with the Nobel Prize for literature, represents an award to a neglected, if not abandoned, body of literature heretofore not given proper recognition by whoever is responsible for the creation of the canonic list of "masterpieces of world literature."

April 1999

The Gypsy Balladeer

T HE CHILEAN POET Pablo Neruda was once asked which were the best and worst language vehicles for his poetry in translation. After pondering the matter, the poet opined that he preferred Italian, since it "comes closest (to my original Spanish), because by keeping the values of the words, the sound helps reflect the sense." English was deemed the worst for his purposes, "being so much more direct, [it] often expresses the meaning of my poetry but does not convey its atmosphere." Indeed, the poet added, "the accuracy of the translation itself, of the meaning, may be what destroys the poem." It should be noted that the French language did not fare well, either: "In many of the French translations . . . my poetry seems to me to vanish, nothing is left, yet one can't complain because they express what one has written." Translation is clearly a complex problem, best summarized by the impression that a whole range of poetic expression in Spanish has an emotional charge and a verbal power best realized by reading the poetry aloud, as most certainly is the case with both Neruda and Lorca—their verses take flight only with the spoken word, and their respective public triumphs were often in theaters, if not stadiums (as in Neruda's case). English poetic expression is far more muted, *pace* Dylan Thomas, more for the eye than the ear. One only has to compare and contrast any of the recordings made by Neruda and T. S. Eliot to hear the most convincing testimony on this matter.

The poetry of Federico García Lorca has offered similar challenges to a translator from Spanish to English over the years. It cannot be just happenstance that Ted Hughes, exasperated after the near impossible task of translating García Lorca's stark tragedy *Bodas De Sangre* into *Blood Wedding*, pronounced in definitive fashion that "Lorca cannot be Englished." All the more compliments and salutations are therefore due to the eminent Lorca scholar Christopher Maurer for bringing out this year, some sixty-six years after the poet's gruesome assassination near his home in Granada, the first almost complete bilingual edition of the Lorca corpus,* with many previously uncollected and unpublished poems translated here for the first time. The volume is "almost complete" due to the fact that the editor has thankfully given us only a brief selection from Lorca's first collection, *The Book of Poems*, the poet's lengthiest book and easily the worst, plain and simple. Indeed, it is difficult to glimpse the future in this mass of poetic mediocrity,

---

* *Collected Poems*, by Federico García Lorca, edited by Christopher Maurer (Farrar, Straus & Giroux).

but Lorca was soon to find his voice with *Poem of the Deep Song*, and after that, there was no stopping him—that is, until Franco's goons rounded him up along with every other local free-thinking university professor, liberal town councilor, the odd Mason and the local Homais, doctors, teachers, humble workers, and trade unionists. Before Lorca was shot in late August 1936, some 280 citizens had suffered the same fate in the same place.

Professor Maurer has given us a short literary history of Lorca's poetic development, and there are so many disparate elements synthesized therein that summary is well nigh impossible. Probably the surest way to start is by realizing that Lorca, a good pianist, came to literature from music—a hovering presence over all of Lorca's life is the saintly figure of Manuel de Falla, a mentor in every sense of the word. In 1922, just at the start of Lorca's meteoric career, the poet and the composer organized a one-time only Festival of Cante Jondo, more popularly known as "flamenco," where distinguished artists and instrumentalists were presented well away from smelly bars and dives—both poet and musician were arguing for the musical and poetic identity of Andalusia, a minuscule patch of land that reached out somehow to Bizet, Glinka, Rimsky-Korsakov, Ravel, and Debussy. The festival transformed a provinciality into a universality—gypsies, bullfighters, singers emblematic of everyman are known throughout the world today through Lorca's poetic mythification.

In spite of the renown, ever since Bizet's *Carmen*, of

a generalized Andalusian atmosphere, it is important to emphasize how intensely Lorca fought against the cheapest and most touristic kind of folklore. He was nothing if not an all-embracing poet, fusing the past (going right back to the metaphorical daring evident in the Muslim poets of the Caliphate) and on to a complete re-evaluation of traditional folk poetry, as dramatized by the epochal researches and recordings made by Ramón Menéndez Pidal. But just as he was a devourer and assimilator of Andalusia's past, and Granada's past in particular, he had a thirst for the future of literature—his friendships with Pablo Neruda and, above all, to Salvador Dalí were emblematic—each successive book of Lorca was a new beginning, a break with the most recent innovation. The aesthetic and qualitative distance between the *Book of Poems* and the *Poem of the Deep Song* is stunning, inexplicable. But as he moves through the twenties, each book, the *Suites*, the *Songs*, and the culminating *Romancero gitano* (Gypsy Ballads) are each exercises in condensation, metaphorical daring, imposition of mystery, and, above all, avoidance of the abstract within a constant contemplation of death. Lorca prided himself on his instinctive imagination, his anti-academic poetic prowess, even though his literary essays, above all those on Gongora, children's nursery songs, and imagination versus inspiration, are splendidly argued and carefully developed. He was a bear of a worker—dead at thirty-eight, he had written thirteen plays and nine books of verse, plus numerous other essays, interviews, and a rich varia.

Professor Maurer's splendid edition is all the more treasured because we can finally take the measure of the poet, now well away from the circumstances of his death and his inevitable transfiguration into *the* tragic symbol of the death of the Spanish republic. In many ways, his death prevented a close reading of his complete achievement, and his flamboyant personality often got in the way too. For instance, Jorge Luis Borges met Lorca in 1933 in Buenos Aires; it was not a happy encounter. In a not atypical burst of savagery, Borges recalled Lorca only by saying that "I suppose he had the good luck to be executed, no? He struck me as a kind of play actor, no? Living up to a certain role, I mean being a professional Andalusian." Borges, who by then was gradually transforming himself into an Eliotic, metaphysical poet, was appalled by the very gay flair of the lionized poet, along with the increasingly vanguardistic daring of Lorca's work, evident above all in his *Poet in New York*, and he was pitiless in his estimation of Lorca, before and after his death.

Twelve translators have participated in this estimable effort, and in general I found the versions to be not only accurate but also attentive to the quality of the poem as a poem in English. The distance between Spanish poetic practice and the general tone of English poetry today demands a kind of associative and freely engaged reader. For a reader only familiar with Lorca's "greatest hits," many of the poems of the middle period have a Haiku-like intensity and economy that is not often associated with the Lorca of a more rhetorical thrust such as that typified by the *Gypsy Ballads* or *The Poet in New York*, the latter work finally published posthumously in 1940. Here is one of my favorites, a Haiku translated by Alan S. Trueblood from Lorca's *Songs, 1921–1924*:

Despedida (Leave-taking)

If I die,
leave the balcony open.
The boy is eating oranges.
(From my balcony I can see him.)
The reaper is reaping the wheat.
(From my balcony I can hear him.)
If I die,
leave the balcony open!

October 2002

Fantastic Argentine

GENERALIZATIONS about contemporary writing from Spanish America are neither advisable nor recommended for general use. There is nothing coherent to be said about the literary production of twenty distinct countries, where the situation of the writer, the place accorded literature in that society, and the author's particular response to the societal and political mix are a special case in each instance, applicable not even to a neighboring country. This is so in spite of the fact that Spanish American authors all seem to write in the same language and have a common history of conquest, colonization, and apparent liberation from the political and cultural models that were Spain's legacy from the age of discovery. Though such things are not known or acknowledged in the U.S.A., it is good to keep in mind that an Argentine arriving in Mexico is a Martian to most Mexicans, as is a Cuban arriving in Chile—utterly different worlds on all fronts. All the more reason for insisting on specificity when talking about a particular author today.

For instance, within the Peruvian context, where literature is rarely granted any distance from society, and where fiction is more likely to be valued for its documentary value than for its imaginative qualities, it was logical that Mario Vargas Llosa would feel compelled to offer his candidacy for the presidency of Peru. Vargas Llosa is a devourer of reality, a manic Flaubertian, scrutinizing and exposing the fossilized structures of Peru's authoritarian feudalism. But unlike Flaubert (although similar to other Peruvian writers before him), he possesses a messianic compulsion to cure the nation of its ills by his own magisterial hand—a vocation for martyrdom. Writers turning into politicians and failing miserably are an old story in parts of Spanish America, and literature is not the better for these dalliances. In any case, it was a Peruvian phenomenon, not readily replicable elsewhere. For instance, a "committed" writer such as the Colombian Gabriel García Márquez, who apparently has ideas similar to those of Vargas Llosa, has always insisted that the only social responsibility of the writer is to write well, and that's that. He has consistently refused (and there have been many) offers of ambassadorships, consulates, and possible candidacies for the presidency of Colombia. He's been wise to do so.

If generalizations are perforce shaky, it is nonetheless true that the North American reader does have an *impression* of and about contemporary fiction from Spanish America, more likely than not drawn from a recent and cursory reading of a few works of, say, García Márquez or Isabel Allende. Such an impression, nebulous and vague as it is, is widespread, and it always seems to point to a kind of performance practice which distinguishes Spanish American fiction from its North American counterpart, and this in turn relates to the uses and misuses of the fantastic. It would seem that most American readers are under the impression that the only mode practiced in Spanish America is something called "magic realism," or, to use another term, coined by the Cuban novelist Alejo Carpentier, "the marvelous real." The two terms mean quite different things, but no matter; for the North American reader, the terms have come to be equivalent. García Márquez's *One Hundred Years of Solitude* is the touchstone for this visionary literature. Examples abound therein. Along with the many gory and exorbitant events in that novel, Father Nicanor Reyna levitates twelve centimeters above the ground upon sipping a cup of chocolate, while Remedios the Beautiful is swept up into the heavens accompanied by a gaggle of airborne bedsheets.

MANY READERS have taken these magical episodes as examples of a piquant fancy, suggestive of the author's addiction to medieval chronicles and chivalric novels. This is very much to the point, since García Márquez has always expressed his contempt for slice-of-life literature and for European realism in general, and has tended to veer toward adventure stories, fairy tales, and children's literature as nurturing elements for his own writing—the world of the romance. Most occasional readers of Spanish American fiction have taken this style as the coin of the realm, as if fantasy, hyperbole, and dream were always present.

Historically, just the reverse is the case. Since the first recognizable novel in all of the colonies was not published until 1816 in Mexico, the founding novels of the nineteenth century in each of the newly independent nations were born under the successive novelistic aesthetics of what then reigned in France and Spain—romanticism, realism, and, markedly, naturalism. In these novels, Nature itself—or rather the unequal contention between man and nature—was the protagonist. Zola was a hidden master behind these novels, which came in many guises and have had many labels in the histories of the Spanish American novel—the "novel of the earth," "the protest novel," "the *indianista* novel," "the novel of the Mexican Revolution"—and they carried on a hardy existence in across the continent until well into the 1940s. García Márquez, whose grand novel was published as recently as 1967, was one of the first of today's writers to lament the persistence of parochial realism in Spanish America. Things could have been quite different in terms of literary evolution had Spanish American writers reached back to pre-nineteenth-century, even medieval, models:

The authors of chivalric novels succeeded in inventing a world in which the imagination was possible. The only important thing for them was the validity of the account, and if they deemed it necessary for the knight to have his head cut off four times, it would be

cut off four times. This amazing capacity for inventing fables penetrated the reader of that period in such
a way that it became the emblem of the conquest of
America. The sad part is that Latin American literature should have forgotten so soon about its marvelous origins.

If García Márquez and his contemporaries (Alejo
Carpentier, Julio Cortázar, Carlos Fuentes, and Mario
Vargas Llosa, to name a few) represent the new canon
that has spead *urbi et orbi* throughout college curricula
as "representative" of the Spanish American novel, the
old canon survives only as a subject for revisionist
readings and an exemplar of historical interest.

One of the main agents in displacing the old with
the new was the Argentine novelist and essayist
Adolfo Bioy Casares. Born in 1914 in Buenos Aires,
he found himself in such fortunate financial circumstances that he was able to dedicate himself to a
writing career, with the passionate encouragement of
his littérateur father. His older friend and compatriot
Jorge Luis Borges (b. 1899) had similar luck—a well-
off family and a father who, frustrated by his own
lack of literary talent, poured his unrealized ambitions
into his son. The two met for the first time in 1932,
and although they were always to be quite different as
writers, a unique friendship developed over the years
which resulted not only in their reviewing and com-
menting upon each other's literary production, but
also in their jointly creating a "third party," an author
dubbed "*Biorges*" by one of Borges's biographers.

The two collaborated in five works of fiction, most of them parodies of detective stories modeled on their avid readings in Chesterton and Conan Doyle. They also produced (with Silvina Ocampo) an anthology which was to make its mark on the future of much of Spanish American writing, the *Anthology of Fantastic Literature* (1940), where Lewis Carroll abuts Cocteau, Alexandra David-Néel, and Kafka, and Lord Dunsany finds himself in the company of Chuang-Tzu, Saki, and Swedenborg. The editors included one of Borges's finest early short stories, "Tlön, Uqbar, Orbis Tertius" (where Bioy Casares appears as a literary character on the first page of the story—the purported reader of the false, pirated encyclopedia which in due course gives birth to the invading planet Tlön). Bioy Casares also put his name on the truculent prologue to the anthology, which is as much a manifesto as anything else. He there notes that in "Tlön, Uqbar, Orbis Tertius" Borges "created a new literary genre, part essay, part fiction. This new genre of Borges is an exercise in a rigorously applied intelligence and felicitous imagining, a story without padding, without the 'human element,' neither emotional nor heart-rending, all aimed at intellectual readers, students of philosophy, some specialists in literature."

IN A SIMILAR VEIN, Borges and Bioy Casares, during a long conversation one afternoon in 1939, compiled a list "of what was to be avoided in literature." The anathemata included "works in which the real protagonist was the pampa, the virgin jungle, the sea, a deluge, or monetary profit," or "works which have situations with which the reader identifies," or "works which pretend to be menus, albums, itineraries, musical concerts"; also, works "which ask for illustration, which suggest films." It should be added that Borges and his friend had the good sense to pull their own legs and include, in their list of prohibitions, works which "include in their plot development vain plays with time and space as found in Faulkner, Borges, and Bioy." During this same conversation, Borges described to Bioy Casares the outline of one of his finest literary spoofs, "Pierre Menard, Author of the Quixote."

Throughout the groves of academe, more than a few doctoral dissertations are surely in preparation concerning the multiple significance of this friendship, which ended only with the death of Borges in 1986. In his "Autobiographical Essay," Borges recognized the complexity of their relationship and made a telling remark about the debt he felt he owed to the younger writer:

> It has always been taken for granted in these cases that the elder man is the master and the younger his disciple. This may have been true at the outset but several years later, when we began to work together, Bioy was really and secretly the master. . . . Opposing my taste for the emotional, the sententious and the baroque, Bioy made me feel that quietness and restraint are more desirable. If I may be allowed a sweeping statement, Bioy led me gradually to classicism.

As Borges's biographer Emir Rodríguez Monegal noted in his lengthy discussion of the relationship, Bioy Casares published his most famous work, *The Invention of Morel*, with a prologue by Borges, just a few weeks before the publication of the "fantastic" anthology in November 1940. Like Bioy's manifesto for the anthology, Borges's prologue to his friend's work rails against the psychological novel in general and its most particular manifestation—the Russian novel, with Dostoevsky probably the principal target. Borges finds such novels to be loose, baggy monsters, as did Henry James, but in terms unique to his own perception of the nature of literature: "The Russians and their disciples have demonstrated, tediously, that nobody is impossible. A person may kill himself because he is so happy, for example, or commit murder as an act of benevolence. And one man can inform on another out of fervor or humility. In the end, such complete freedom is tantamount to chaos." Turning to Bioy Casares's rigorously plotted novel, he places it on a level of achievement equal to any other work of the time or of the previous few decades:

> I believe I am free from every superstition of modernity, or any illusion that yesterday differs intimately from today or will differ from tomorrow; but I maintain that during no other era have there been novels with such admirable plots as *The Turn of the Screw*, *Der Prozess*, *Le voyageur sur la terre* (of Julien Green), and the one you are about to read, which was written by Adolfo Bioy Casares.

A selection from the fiction of Bioy Casares has just been published by New Directions.* The deft translator of these stories, Suzanne Jill Levine, points out in her introduction that while H. G. Wells's novel *The Island of Dr. Moreau* (1896) provided the point of departure for Bioy Casares, *The Invention of Morel* should not be taken as mere science fiction. Alfred Mac Adam described *Morel* as "a text about a man who becomes first an artist and then a work of art." The plot is simple: a fugitive, shipwrecked on an island, spies on an alluring group of elegant vacationers who fill their days with drink, fine talk, a good selection of records of the Twenties, and innumerable games of tennis. He soon becomes enamored of the *belle dame* of the group, Faustine. As he observes all of them over a period of weeks without his presence being noted, he realizes that they repeat every conversation, every move and gesture, cyclically over a fixed stretch of time. They have died, or have been killed, after having been filmed in three dimensions by the sinister group leader, Morel. Finally concluding that what he sees is a kind of continuous holographic film loop whose projected images have bulk and move about the island as if alive, the fugitive determines to master Morel's invention (powered by the fluctuation of the tides) so that he will be able to intercalate himself into this revolving time machine of images. He wants to stand (or lie) next to the already pre-

---

* *Selected Stories*, by Adolfo Bioy Casares, translated by Suzanne Jill Levine (New Directions).

programed Faustine, who will of course never know of his presence. Intimacy will be denied him, but the anguishing approximation of it is better than nothing. The young lover forever on the brink of possession, encased in a work of art, has some consolations —Keats's "Ode on a Grecian Urn" being the classic formulation.

Bioy Casares's brief novel represents the proto-artist who is at once writing in a diary (inscribing on the urn, if you will) and making himself into a component part of (and a collaborator on) an art object, a permanence of images. *The Invention of Morel* is one of the first instances of a movement away from representation in literature in Spanish America. By the way, the work attracted the attention of Alain Robbe-Grillet, who reviewed it in *Critique* in 1953; it can be seen as a sub-text to his screenplay for the film *Last Year at Marienbad* (1961). Robbe-Grillet admitted to as much in an interview. He tells how, after the première of the film, a friend (Claude Ollier) called to congratulate him on his achievement, but began with a memorable exclamation: "Mais, c'est L'Invention de Morel!" At any rate, Bioy Casares has hardly been idle since then. Aside from the collaborations with Borges, he has published some fifteen books—novels, novellas, and short stories—along with a number of critical articles in Argentine journals; he has also continued on as a some-time anthologist. One of his more mordant works of recent years is his *Dictionary of the Exquisite Argentine* (second edition, 1990), a compilation of barbarisms and pompous anglicisms that have crept into daily use in Buenos Aires. The growing corruption of meaning in daily language usage has always been a major concern.

By now it is probably impossible to extricate the name of Bioy Casares from its association with Borges and his work. They are, howevever, quite distinct writers, though they both share a penchant for the metaphysical and the sense of life-out-of-mind-and-body. But Borges always had a leaning toward the epic sense of life, what with his celebration of Walt Whitman, his addiction to the major films of the "Western" genre, his espousal of *Ulysses*, his avoidance of the intimate tone, his real aversion to the confessional aspects of literary expression. On the contrary, Bioy Casares "tends toward the lyrical," in the words of Ms. Levine, with a special attention to Baudelaire, Rimbaud, and especially Verlaine, authors who find little favor indeed in Borges's eccentric pantheon. Furthermore, Bioy Casares's stories flow in realms that Borges would never acknowledge as proper for his own writing.

All of the pieces in the present collection are taken from four books dating from the mid-1950s through the late 1980s; they revolve around the subject of love, which manifests itself in a hallucinatory and obsessive way within each story. Most of the pieces are variations on the theme of *l'amour fou*, described in an offhand and oblique way that makes each character something of a phantom, a mental event rather than an evolving person on the page.

The most intriguing thread running through these

stories is the repetition of a kind of child's adventure tale, only eroticized: each story rehearses a search for the beloved across space and time which more often than not ends in grinding frustration and a hallucinatory dénouement. Bioy Casares's art draws upon the world of the child as a diagram for the deceptions and disillusions of adulthood. Still, the child remaining within always has the option of returning home to the cozy world of uncomplicated parental affection. In a brief chronology of his life written in 1975, Bioy Casares recalls that in early childhood, at around age five, "my mother [told] me stories about animals who stray from the nest, are exposed to danger, and in the end, after many adventures, return to the security of the nest. The theme of the safe, or apparently safe, haven, out of the dangers that lurk outside still (in 1975) appeals to me." The way this plays out is elusive; the stories tell of events in a monochromatic stream of time without much tonal variation or carefully prefigured surprises within the ongoing flow of things. The machismo of the errant male, a favorite target, is subverted, put at a loss, while women's sensibilities and questing are no luckier but are seen in an immensely more generous light. Like the protagonist of *The Invention of Morel*, Bioy Casares's people are losers, they are always out of joint. Often physically together, "adjoining" each other as it were, they are at an unbreachable psychic distance.

For instance, in "Women Are All The Same," a young wife, over the objections of her much younger suitor, allows her elderly husband to intern her in an insane asylum, thereby "achieving security," suggests Ms. Levine, "by making fidelity into a form of suicide." In "Men Are All The Same," an adoring friend of a young widow loses out to a much younger man, whom in turn she finally discovers to have an interest in her only because of the splendid automobile she lets him drive. In "Pearls Before Swine," a passionate attachment of one woman only casually answered by an inattentive friend is discovered by that same suitor to have been the romantic "love of his life," far too many years late. In "Dorotea," a man's search for his estranged wife in the south of France ends in his finding his daughter, but not his wife. She has died, and the daughter is now unreachable and distant. What might have been ends in frustration and isolation. Bioy Casares's fluent manipulation of time and space is evident in "About the Shape of the World" and "The Hero of Women," but these are not "escapist" pieces; the political realities of Argentina intrude throughout. "The Myth of Orpheus and Eurydice" is based on the torching of Buenos Aires's elegant Jockey Club by enraged *Peronistas*. Inside the political anecdote, the story tells of a dramatic and failed search for love as the hordes plunder this bastion of the old aristocracy. As in Borges, dream is the bedrock of Bioy Casares's reality. Ms. Levine quotes Borges to good effect on this matter: "Nobody knows whether the world is a natural process or whether it is a kind of dream which we may or may not share with others."

Robbe-Grillet said of *The Invention of Morel* that it was "un livre étonnant," which might be variously translated as an "astonishing" or "amazing book." It is most certainly that—a revelation—and should be read anew by every generation. The stories in this collection, however, are not at that level of intensity; they artfully echo Bioy Casares's major achievement of 1940, exploring the obsessions implicit in the earlier masterpiece. Still, that should be more than enough to explain why Bioy Casares is now Argentina's most distinguished living man of letters and is considered a founding father of the new novel in all of Spanish America. When Carlos Fuentes noted that "without Borges, there would be no new Spanish American novel," he misspoke—he should have said "*Biorges.*"

October 1994

Part Two

The Sibelius Question

THE MUSICAL REPUTATION of the Finnish composer Jean Sibelius (1865–1957)—deified in the Twenties and Thirties by conductors and public alike, declining markedly in the Forties, and hitting a very deep bottom from the Fifties on—has taken another turn. His shares are up. There is now once more a Sibelius Question. No such thing as a Stravinsky Question or even a Schoenberg Question troubles the sleep of music critics: their respective reputations are secure for the time being.

The renewed controversy about the musical viability and the simple quality of Sibelius's music was the subject of a series of performances and a symposium in December 1997 at Avery Fisher Hall titled "Northern Lights: The Music of Jean Sibelius." Sir Colin Davis and the London Symphony performed three concerts of five of the seven symphonies of the Finnish master, plus a few tone poems and some songs for soprano and orchestra. His less abundant chamber music was represented by a recital by the Lark Quartet, assisted by the pianist Samuel Sanders. The two-week survey featuring intermittent concerts and discussions ended with a lieder recital of Sibelius's songs by the baritone Jorma Hynninen.

In addition to this musical overview, there was an all-day symposium on December 6 under the general aegis of Professor James Hepokoski of the University of Minnesota.* Professor Hepokoski gathered together eminent Sibelians from the United Kingdom, Finland, and the United States to ponder such topics as "The Development of a Voice: Influences on Sibelius," "Controversies Surrounding Sibelius," and "The Legacy of Sibelius." The upshot: over the figurative dead bodies of Igor Stravinsky and Arnold Schoenberg, Sibelius's music still commands a large and fervent audience. What is more surprising, his works are having a considerable effect on contemporary compositional habits—in the work of John Adams, for instance—and this in turn has to do with something like a reaction against the "progressive," more or less atonal language of what was the dominant mode of compositional expression for decades after the Second World War, an admixture of Stravinsky, Schoenberg, Webern, Alban Berg, and Béla Bartók.

As is the habit among academics, the personality and character of Sibelius himself were held at arm's length—and this is understandable, for even during

---

* "The Sibelius Symposium," featuring James Hepokoski, Glenda Dawn Goss, Matti Huttunen, Robert Layton, Alex Ross, Robert Spano, and others, was held at the Stanley Kaplan Penthouse, Lincoln Center, New York, on December 6, 1997.

the composer's lifetime he was notoriously diffident about his own world view and absolutely silent about his compositional methods. He had nothing to say to conductors when they came to ask advice about how his music should be played. (Finally in 1943, he did supply metronome indications for his scores at the behest of conductors but remained mute on stylistic points.) Sibelius had pretty tough things to say about recordings of his work, above all as directed by British conductors—Sir Thomas Beecham, for instance—who advertised themselves as "specialists" in Sibelius. More of this later.

When someone from the audience at the symposium asked about Sibelius's intellectual formation, his core philosophical beliefs, his readings, there was absolute silence. The experts had nothing to say on the matter, though there was some mention about his being a "pantheist" and something of a "mystic." Indeed, there was a certain aspect in Sibelius that might respond to such a description. Gifted with perfect pitch, he associated certain colors with certain notes and at times key signatures, and did so from earliest childhood. When his secretary Santeri Levas asked him what his favorite color was, Sibelius responded by saying that "it is a clear green, somewhere between D and E-flat." According to Levas, "Then he sang that note to me and went to the piano to check it. He had got it exactly. For the D (on the piano) was a shade lower than the note he had sung, and the E-flat noticeably higher."

Sibelius always knew that he would be cursed with

longevity: "In a meeting I once said that everybody who was there would be dead before me. Naturally they protested that no one could know that precisely. . . . I knew it with complete certainty, and they're all long since dead." His dream-life was especially rich.

> Once he spent some months in Japan (in a dream), although the period of dreaming was limited to hours. In the morning he even remembered that his correspondence (from Finland) was forwarded to him from a *poste restante* and that each day he fetched his letters from the post office. He dreamed a great deal about Japan, although he had never been there. . . . In other dreams about Japan, he was always in the same large square, but new buildings appeared that had not been there in earlier dreams.

Sibelius was also something of a psychic, and often frightened and astonished those close to him when these divinations were expressed.

And then there is the matter of his carefully-groomed personal appearance. As the founding father of the expression of Finnish nationalism in epic musical terms, Sibelius always cultivated in his maturity and old age the granitic appearance of the dour, heroic Finn, symbolic of his nation's recent history, its struggle for independence from Russia above all. Although painted portraits of the composer as a young man show him with a fiery red head of hair, he carefully shaved whatever was left and made sure that he looked more and more sculpted and stony as he aged.

This desired image was confirmed by the famous chiaroscuro black-and-white photographic portrait of Sibelius with eyes closed, taken by "Karsh of Ottowa" in 1949, by now the most disseminated image of the composer.

ALTHOUGH most of the participants in the symposium, out of decency and reverence, did not want to mention particular personal traits of the composer, it is well known that he drank like a fish and would carouse with friends for days on end. Absenting himself from his family for more than a few lost weekends, he caused much anguish for his wife, Aino, and their five daughters. He was maniacally extravagant, had a household of five servants, and was constantly hounded by debts, although a governmental honorific pension granted in 1897 did ease things a bit. He had a very bad case of hand tremor, which a few think may have been at least partly responsible for his curtailed career as a composer.

The overwhelming fact about the life of Jean Sibelius is its sheer span. Born in 1865 into a Swedish-speaking family (Finnish was an acquired second language), Sibelius was something of a late bloomer as a student violinist and composer. He was in Vienna by 1891, received gruffly but with distant admiration by Johannes Brahms. He also conversed with and gave work to a very old man who had been Beethoven's piano tuner. His tone poems *En Saga* (1892) and *Finlandia* (1899), together with his first symphony (1899), had established his reputation as a musical innovator by the turn of the century. He was treated as an equal by Gustav Mahler in an impassioned meeting and conversation in 1907, and was championed by both Richard Strauss and Ferruccio Busoni. Enthusiasm for his work grew both in England and in the United States, with performances by Karl Muck and Max Fiedler in Boston—all of this well before the Great War.

In the Twenties, Sibelius's place in the vanguard had slipped. His works faced increasingly stiff competition and criticism from such composers as Stravinsky and Schoenberg, whose respective revolutionary musical languages had been well-established prior to the war with Schoenberg's *Pierrot Lunaire* (1912) and Stravinsky's *Rite of Spring* (1913). Faced with the incessant propaganda by these composers' critical and conductorial minions—and sensing that these musical developments could not be incorporated into his own very original manner of organizing and displaying sound in the orchestra—Sibelius essentially withdrew from the contemporary music scene only to undergo the torture of living too long, all of ninety-two years. Sibelius's last major works were the Symphony No. 7 (1924) and the tone poem he wrote for the conductor Walter Damrosch in New York, *Tapiola* (1925). His death in 1957 put an end to a creative silence that had lasted some thirty-two years. Indeed, so unsure of his gifts had he become that Sibelius almost didn't send *Tapiola*, his last masterpiece. By all accounts, there did exist finished movements for an Eighth Symphony, but, despite endless importuning from conductors and impresarios, Sibelius threw what he had finished of the work, along with a laundry basket full of other manuscripts, into a furnace in the mid-Forties.

Sibelius and his silence after 1925 were the inevitable subject of speculations on the part of the participants in the symposium. Much emphasis was put on his ever-increasing self-criticism, on how he would destructively brood over negative reviews while taking no delight in praise. Conversely, the positive reception of his last two works from the mid-Twenties may have instilled doubts as to whether he ever could do any better. The destructive element finally won over the creative, but even leaving off composition gave him no peace. As Sibelius said to Santeri Levas, "Heaven on earth begins when man forsakes self-criticism." Since there would be no more works to self-criticize, an earthly heaven might have been unconsciously awaited by the composer after he essentially abandoned writing serious music. But as the years dragged on and national adulation turned to worldwide deification—and as he compulsively kept on working under this severe sense of inadequacy—the possible portrait of a happily silent composer never could be drawn. It cannot have been easy: living as a national monument when one is already a statue.

Another prior instance of creative silence—the thirty-nine years left to Gioacchino Rossini after the composition of *William Tell* (1829)—is another matter. Rossini had done all that he wanted to do and thought he *could* do. Consequently, he decided to pack it in, travel around Europe in his carriage adorned with innumerable bells, and enjoy life. He did write some piano pieces and wind music, but his opera writing was finished.

Leaving these thoughts aside, there was a recurring subtext to the symposium and to the informative notes supplied by Professor Hepokoski for the program booklet accompanying the symphony performances by Sir Colin Davis and the London Symphony. This subtext had nothing to do with Sibelius or his work, but it did have a lot to do with the political-cultural warfare of the Twenties and Thirties and the history of musical modernism. In short, Sibelius gradually came to be considered the bandleader of musical conservatism. For his many critics, he was a composer who wanted to have it both ways—to be both modern and traditional. Of the younger generation from the 1920s, Paul Hindemith might be taken as a figure who represented this tendency to some degree. Arnold Schoenberg himself never hid his contempt for such compositional compromises, since he saw himself as a genius whose musical language corresponded exactly to the necessities and exigencies of the age into which he was born—the generation after Mahler and Strauss. It was a matter of historical inevitability; the step had to be taken. Schoenberg was not above a witticism on the matter: "The middle way is the only road that *doesn't* lead to Rome."

At the symposium, in a clever pedagogical strategy, Professor Hepokoski played the devil's advocate *against* Sibelius, reciting succinctly the arguments put forth by the avant-garde against the composer. For a start, Sibelius was a holdover from the Romantic age; he was "expressive" in the old sense and utterly devoid of ironic reference. He was obviously incapable of learning creatively from Schoenberg, Stravinsky, or anyone else, and this was why he folded his tent: he couldn't survive as an equal among the Young Turks. On a darker plane, the criticism mentioned the fact that the mystical, neo-pagan *Naturgefühl* emanating from Sibelius's music found an echo in the "blood and soil" atmosphere of Aryan cultural superiority then rampant in Germany. The fact that Sibelius did not reject a Goethe prize proferred by Hitler and was cultivated by Goebbels was an index, his critics averred, of how pernicious were the forces represented by his music. The new music, his opponents went on to say, is urban, intimately related to technology, the life of the city, the free consciousness in total experimentation with new sounds and new materials. Sibelius was a throwback to a musical barbarism.

This was war. And, as Dr. Kissinger informs us, in war there are winners and losers. Among the cognoscenti, Sibelius lost. Let it be said that the anti-Sibelius forces in Europe and in the United States were a formidable lot. They had blistering artillery manned by such good soldiers as Theodor W. Adorno, René Leibowitz, Nadia Boulanger, Virgil Thomson, and B. H. Haggin, among others.

The arguments against Sibelius that the Frankfurt School Marxist Theodor Adorno put forward are a good case in point. In his *Philosophy of Modern Music* (1949), "Glosses on Sibelius," and elsewhere, Adorno portrayed Sibelius as a classic cultural product for the masses, "the ideal of Aunt Jemima's ready-mix for pancakes extended to the field of music." Sibelius, according to Adorno, reinforced the musical status quo, as did the radio broadcasts of Toscanini (who included in his programs a good dose of Sibelius): "the ruined farmer is consoled by the radio-instilled belief that Toscanini is playing for him and for him alone, and that an order of things that allows him to hear Toscanini compensates for low market prices for farm products." In "Glosses on Sibelius," Adorno categorically states that "if Sibelius's music is good music, then all categories by which musical standards can be measured—standards which reach from a master like Bach to the most advanced composers like Schoenberg—must be completely abolished." For Adorno, as a self-ordained theoretician of the "progressive," it was the heroic figure of Arnold Schoenberg who brought the Mosaic tablets with the new laws to direct the practice of all future generations of composers. Any adherence to tonality was treason in the light of this new bit of musical history in the making.

Similar thoughts were voiced by René Leibowitz, author of *Schoenberg and His School*. In 1955, Leibowitz composed a two-page "homage" to Sibelius on the occasion of the composer's ninetieth birthday. This short work carried the grateful title of "Sibelius: The Worst Composer in the World." The arguments were Adornian. The marketing of Sibelius had been similar to the flogging of automobiles, cigarettes, and toothpaste. Complaining about the "incorrect" harmony, the monotony of the music, the lack of polyphony, Leibowitz informed us that the impression of originality that Sibelius's works give is due to "ignorance, incompetence and impotence." Furthermore, Sibelius's success is due to a misguided hope that one can make new music with the old means. "The only merit of Sibelius is to show us in magisterial fashion that the old means, which were authentic enough for their times, are false for the present, and that, by using these old means now, nothing is easier than to become the worst composer in the world." Sibelius himself never indulged in such dogmatic anathemas. He studied the early works of Schoenberg under the guidance of Busoni, admired his orchestral craft but admittedly didn't like the sound. He had good words for Stravinsky and Shostakovich, but reserved his highest esteem for the works of Béla Bartók and Alban Berg, "Schoenberg's greatest achievement," as he once put it.

For defenders of Sibelius, the symposium was an occasion to take appreciative note of recent scholarly contributions by one of the participants in the Sibelius symposium—Professor Glenda Dawn Goss of the University of Georgia. Professor Goss has recently published not only an anthology of critical articles by herself and others on Sibelius, *A Sibelius Companion* (Greenwood Press, 1996), but also a major critical overview of the arguments from the pro-Sibelius faction, *Jean Sibelius and Olin Downes: Music, Friendship, Criticism* (Northeastern University Press, 1994). As reigning musical critic first in Boston for sixteen years, then, more importantly, for *The New York Times* from 1924 until well into the Fifties, Olin Downes was the prime ringleader of the pro-Sibelius forces in the United States. He was active also as a broadcast host for radio concerts by the New York Philharmonic, and was a well-known figure in the burgeoning area of "music appreciation" not only with his broadcasts, but also with lectures on the Chautauqua circuit. Professor Goss's study also includes all of the correspondence between this critic and Sibelius himself. As many music-lovers of an earlier generation will recall, Virgil Thomson was the formidable anti-Sibelius figure at *The New York Herald Tribune*. In his first review for the *Trib*, dated October 11, 1940, Thomson carved up Sibelius's Symphony No. 2, finding it "vulgar, self-indulgent, and provincial beyond all description."

From today's perspective, Downes's language praising Sibelius defies belief. For Downes, the music of Sibelius was a matter of manliness against decadence. "There is no more virile music written today," he stated. Sibelius was a "new, clean, great man." The Symphony No. 2 was "gloriously rude"; its composer was an "unwashed Viking." After hearing Sibelius's *En Saga*, Downes confessed that "when I hear this music I avow a carnal desire to discard the soft fat ways of life; to set out in oilskins, or something, for somewhere, to discover at least a desperate polar bear bent on conflict." There is more. Professor Goss also favors us with rich quotations from Downes's ex-coriations of the avant-garde: Debussy's *La Mer* was composed "by a dreamer lying on his couch in a sumptuously upholstered apartment and puffing blue rings of smoke into the air." Schoenberg's *Five Pieces for Orchestra* was a work "exceedingly unhealthy and disagreeable, having neither the grandeur of cleansing tragedy nor the uplift of a great composition that makes all men akin." Gosh. With such friends as advocates, who needs enemies? Sibelius never had a chance, buried under Downes's bombast. As a pawn in a bigger game, Sibelius was condemned to be merely popular, but never an object for serious scholarly consideration or musicological research.

Sir Colin Davis and his younger compatriot Sir Simon Rattle represent the latest generation of a long tradition of Sibelius advocates within the United Kingdom which began early in the century with the efforts of Sir Granville Bantock, to be quickly followed by Sir Thomas Beecham, Sir John Barbirolli, Sir Malcolm Sargent, Basil Cameron, and Anthony Collins. And as it was the London Symphony Orchestra that Davis was conducting in these Avery Fisher Hall performances, it is worth remembering that they made the first recordings of *any* symphony by Sibelius, directed by the master's friend and sometime disciple Robert Kajanus, in the early Thirties. Moreover, since Davis released on CD format a set of digital recordings of the complete Sibelius symphonies on BMG/RCA Victor with the same orchestra, the concerts at Avery

Fisher Hall seemed somewhat like a coronation for the conductor. There was the fervency of true believers in the audience. The critic from *The New York Times*, Anthony Tommasini, seemed perplexed by the piety of the audience: "That Sibelius has won an ardent following was clear on Sunday afternoon at Avery Fisher Hall. One of the most attentive audiences I have been part of in a long time turned out for the London Symphony Orchestra with Sir Colin Davis conducting, part of a two-week Sibelius festival." How could this be? Tommasini seemed to ask.

THERE WERE a few odd touches in programming that should be mentioned. Symphony No. 1 and Symphony No. 6 were missing, even though they had been played during the Sibelius cycle that Davis and the London Symphony had just completed in November at the Barbican Hall in London. Particularly grievous was the absence of the Symphony No. 1, since it was such a bombshell in the year of its first hearing, 1899. Probably only Shostakovich's Symphony No. 1 can be compared as such a stunning announcement of precocity and great things to come.

As soloist in the Violin Concerto, London got the fiery Anne-Sophie Mutter; New York had to make do with Kyoko Takezawa—an estimable player, to be sure, but not in Mutter's league. Although announced, *The Oceanides*—a tone poem first conducted by Sibelius himself in Norfolk, Connecticut, during his only visit to the United States in 1914—was not played. Instead, *The Swan of Tuonela*—a gratingly popular work—was performed. Even more disappointing was the fact that London audiences got to hear a performance of the *Kullervo* Symphony (1892) —a work that Sibelius never permitted to be performed in full during his lifetime. What a coup it would have been to have had *Kullervo* in New York! But New Yorkers had to do without that, as well.

The performances at Avery Fisher conformed more or less to the approach that Davis has taken in his recent digital recordings of these works with the London Symphony Orchestra—which is another way of saying that high tonal sheen, virtuosity, and ponderous pacing were evident throughout. A few fanatics might mention that Davis recorded all the Sibelius symphonies once before, in versions with the Boston Symphony for the Philips label some twenty years ago. These versions are now available on CD at budget prices. For better and for worse, the differences between the old recordings and these new performances, whether live or recorded, were night and day. Where the BSO versions are almost reckless in their impetuosity and sometimes sloppy and uncouth ensemble work, these new versions are stately, with much slower tempi. The primeval fury in the music has been severely diminished, and one has the sense that Davis has gone soft and lost the driving edge that characterized his earlier traversal of the same material. Too often, he seemed uninvolved or quite possibly just bored after having had an excessively intense contact with such a monochromatic composer as Sibelius, both in the recording studio and in the concert hall.

To end on a historical note: since 1982, the Sibelius estate has relinquished all dominion over the remaining manuscripts and other papers in its possession. Among the mountain of pages hauled over to the University of Helsinki, there was found the original version (1915) of the Symphony No. 5, painfully revised on one occasion and given another definitive form in 1919. The conductor's score for the primitive version has been lost, but all the orchestral parts are intact. The sensational young Finnish provincial orchestra, the Lahti Symphony Orchestra, under its conductor Osmo Vänskä (b. 1953), has just released a compact disc recording containing both the first and the last version of the Symphony No. 5, on the BIS Label (CD 863). This recording offers us a glimpse into the self-critical side of Sibelius, the composer trying to give form and continuity to melodic fragments, cutting and adding, sometimes simply juggling with elements not quite yet in their definitive order. This struggle was the essence of the sacred game that was the act of composition for Sibelius. As for these astonishing performances both of the early and later versions of the Symphony No. 5, they surge and move forward in a way that offers instructive contrast to the more Brahmsian-Elgarian approach of Sir Colin in his present-day readings of the Sibelius symphonies.

February 1998

Berg's Femmes Fatales

In *The Dyer's Hand* (1962), W. H. Auden noted that implausibility is the stuff of opera. Librettists revel in shopworn stage conventions—selected villains and nobles, cross-dressers and crossed identities, fluently managed hide-and-seek, violence and the rough stuff just at the right moment. Few operas take this to the extreme of Alban Berg's *Lulu*. It stretches plausibility and even melodrama to the breaking point. But *Lulu* is more than just an expressionist experiment; it is also a commentary on opera's melodramatic clichés, ironically gesturing toward many an opera past. In a very low bow to Da Ponte and Hofmannsthal, for example, *Lulu* features a "trouser" role.

The libretto was drawn from two dramas by Frank Wedekind. Lulu is a young low life from some German city, without genealogy or credentials. She is called Lulu most of the time, but is also known variously as Eve, Nelly, and Mignon. She exercises the hypnotic, sultry allure commanded by Dietrich's Blue Angel, but is less throaty and mannish; the role is for a coloratura, reaching up to a high D. On the way up in society, her stage demeanor is implacably thoughtless and flighty; on the way down, she is robotic, with ever more perceptible traces of the tragic.

The opera begins in a painter's studio. Lulu is posing. Dr. Goll, her first husband (the first we know about, that is), forces his way into the studio, catching his wife with the aroused portrait painter. The doctor collapses and dies. Lulu promptly marries the painter, who is then apprised by Dr. Schoen, a newspaper tycoon, that Lulu has been Schoen's mistress. The painter, beside himself with jealousy, cuts his throat. Desperate to free himself from Lulu's charms, Dr. Schoen takes his fiancée to see her dance at a cabaret, hoping that Lulu will relinquish her hold on him. Instead, she stalks off the stage and, as a sign of her hypnotic power over him, dictates a letter for Schoen to write out, announcing that his engagement is over.

Lulu is now married to Dr. Schoen. Their ménage includes his son Alwa, a composer besotted with Lulu; the mysterious, decrepit Schigolch—Lulu's protector and a mythic "Father Time" figure—and the Countess Geschwitz, a potential lesbian lover of Lulu (at least in her own mind). In gruesome but comic exasperation—"Thirty years I've labored, and this is my life at home!"—Schoen hands Lulu a pistol for her to kill herself. Instead she finishes off Schoen with five shots. Lulu is arrested and sent to prison. But Countess Geschwitz replaces her. Alwa and Lulu come together, embracing on the same couch where his father bled to death. Lulu hints that she also poisoned the first Mrs. Schoen, Alwa's mother.

The third act begins in Paris in a luxurious salon full of bankers and gamblers. Lulu, more penurious than ever, is in danger of being sold as a prostitute to a Cairene brothel. She and Alwa barely escape from the police. The final scene: a London garret, Lulu, accompanied by the remains of her retinue, has become a streetwalker. She returns successively with a silent professor, a black African prince (who, on his way out, crushes Alwa's skull), and Jack the Ripper, who slashes Lulu and (also on his way out) the ever anguished Geschwitz, who has made futile moves to aid Lulu and who utters a final cry: "Lulu! My angel! Appear once more to me! For I am near, I'm always near. For evermore!" ("Im Ewigkeit!").

This Spring the Metropolitan Opera revived John Dexter's 1979 production. (The first complete performances of the opera at the Met had been given the season after the completed three-act version was first staged in Paris on February 24, 1979). At particular moments during the performances (the sudden death of Dr. Goll right at the beginning of the opera, for instance), titters were heard from the Met audience. Some serious Bergians were perturbed at this disruption of mood, but the grotesqueries of the libretto demonstrate Berg's belief that true seriousness embraces the comic. It is full of slapstick moments, such as Schigolch's wheezy asthma as he climbs the stairs or his banana-peel pratfalls on Dr. Schoen's slippery parquet floors ("Diese Parketten!!").

Given the demonic, stringent nature of the musical organization of the work and its heightened expressive musical vocabulary, the settings must anchor themselves realistically in the atmosphere and *Stimmung* indicated by Wedekind and Berg. The highest compliments must be paid to the Met for its realization. The painter's studio, Lulu's dressing room, the Parisian salon, even the London garret brought home to the audience the nasty and gruesome happenings. The sets at the Met give off that "sticky, perfumed, sultry, unhealthy atmosphere" which Stefan Zweig recalled in his memoir of old Vienna, *The World of Yesterday*, and that is all to the good.

Special praise must also go to the Lulu herself, Christine Schaefer, who, with the slightest of physical presences on the stage, magnetically drew the audience into her heedless and insouciant world. During the two intermissions, I couldn't help but overhear learned comparisons concerning previous Lulus such as Teresa Stratas, Anja Silja, and Evelyn Lear, but there seemed to be general agreement that Ms. Schaefer had at least equalled, and possbily excelled, her predecessors. It was a splendid characterization. Ms. Schaefer's performance perfectly captured the spirit of Berg's female Don Giovanni, hardly needing a "catalogue aria" to brag of her conquests. It is also gratifying to note that this production, almost completely sold out this Spring, will reappear, along with *Wozzeck*, during next season.

One of the constants in the critical commentary about Berg concerns the distance between the affable Viennese aristocrat and the two stories he chose to set to music. Of the thirteen works he left behind at his sudden death on Christmas Eve in 1935, *Wozzeck* and *Lulu* are indisputably his masterpieces. Berg's unhappy service in the Austrian Army is the obvious biographical correlative to *Wozzeck*. But the parallels to *Lulu* are buried deeper.

Berg first saw *Pandora's Box*, one of Wedekind's two Lulu plays, at an intimate local theater in Vienna in 1905 when he was twenty. Tilly Newes (the future Mrs. Frank Wedekind) played Lulu, Wedekind himself was Jack the Ripper, and Karl Kraus played the African prince. The performance made an indelible and overwhelming impression on Berg. Wedekind, along with Freud, was positing an unresolvable conflict between instincts and civilization. In a letter of 1907, Berg noted that "At last we have come to the realization that sensuality is not a weakness . . . rather, it is an immense strength that lies in us—the pivot of all being and thinking. (Yes; all thinking!)." It is not certain that Berg ever saw Louise Brooks in Pabst's film *Pandora's Box* (1929) though, movie buff that he was, it is likely. Wedekind's steamy world went on roiling, with all its implications for explicit sensuous eruptions into civil life, in Berg's head. He started to work on *Lulu* in the late 1920s, suffering constant interruptions and frequent despair of ever finishing.

In 1911, Berg married Helene Nahowski. The nature of their relationship is still an enigma. Husband and wife both connived in the public depiction of an ideal marriage, summed up in a 1965 biography of Berg as "even the man happy enough to have enjoyed the more intimate personal acquaintance of the couple can only have a vague idea what this woman came to mean to him. No one could completely grasp what she meant to the *artist* Alban Berg no less than to the *man*." Perhaps, but one can't help noticing that they were apart a good deal of the time and that Helene rarely accompanied Berg on his increasingly triumphal foreign expeditions after the premiere and attendant publicity concerning *Wozzeck*. She remained behind in Vienna or frequented some of her favorite spas. He wrote to her every day, though, when away. In a way, he feared her; her nephew, describing Helene years later, said that "She wanted to be the only Berg."

During an unaccompanied trip to Prague in 1925, Berg met Alma Mahler Werfel's sister-in-law—that is, Franz Werfel's sister, Hanna Fuchs-Robettin, a married woman with two children, wife of a wealthy industrialist. Six months later, he was back in Prague, this time reassuring the mildly suspicious Helene that "It goes against the grain, really, to have to reassure you about me and Mopinka [Hanna's nickname]." Helene was right to feel uneasy. Hanna Fuchs-Robettin was the love of Berg's life, and his letters to her are cast in a language never directed at his wife. "Not a day passes," he wrote in October 1931, "not half a day, not a night, when I do not think of you, not a week when I am not suddenly flooded by yearning, which submerges all my thoughts and feelings and wishes in an ardor that is not weaker by a breath than that of May 1925." In effect, all of Berg's work after

1925 is secretly touched by this unfulfilled and probably unconsummated romance.

On August 11, 1935, Berg noted in a letter to a
friend that "an insect sting exactly at the lower end of
the backbone led—a crescendo lasting days—to a
frightfully painful abscess that takes away all my
pleasure. At the moment, it seems to be subsiding."
Helene Berg—avaricious, simply cheap, or monstrous,
as the case may be—had operated on the cyst at the
base of her husband's spine with a sterilized (she
thought) nail file or scissors, thereby saving a trip to
the doctor. They would never consult a doctor or sur-
geon, and by December Berg was in the filthy general
ward of a local hospital, suffering from severe blood
poisoning. He died on Christmas Eve.

Lulu was left with a small number of measures un-
orchestrated. Helene would never allow a complete
performance of the opera, and that first peformance
in 1979 followed hard on her death in 1976. The
more the listener moves into the central psychic concerns of *Lulu*, the closer we are to the deepest drives
of Berg's own creativity, hidden as it was by his surface life—his own treatment of the conflict between
bourgeois custom and order against feeling and sexual
passion—Wedekind again. Thus, the essence of Berg
lies in the opposition between opposing selves, with
multiple ramifications. As George Perle puts it, "on
the one hand, an extraordinary intensity of feeling,
and on the other, an unprecedented abstraction and
rigor in the musical design, in the working out of
musical ideas, and in the very shape of the themes."

In the structure and casting of the dramatis personae of *Lulu*, there are a series of clever recapitulations and duplications. Thus, Dr. Schoen also takes on the role of Jack the Ripper, the painter later takes on the role of the African Prince, etc. There is an avenging symmetry here. The musical materials are continually recapitulated and recast; these musical leitmotivs have particular effect in act three where they recall Lulu's fabulous past.

As for Berg's "eternal beloved," he had already carefully planted an indication of his love in his "Lyric Suite"—the musical equivalents of the initials HF (Hanna Fuchs, of course) and AB are the key structural elements (H, pronounced "ha," is B natural in German musical spelling) as revealed by George Perle in a 1977 article—without Helene being aware. (Berg also gave Hanna a richly annotated printed pocket score of the work, done with inks of various colors.) And so, it was utterly inevitable that it would be finally revealed (thanks again to George Perle) that the final chord of *Lulu*, sounding after Countess Geschwitz's avowal of eternal love for Lulu beyond the grave, would have, as its lowest note F, and as the highest in the chord H, Berg once again indicating in music that Hanna Fuchs would remain with him as long as he lived and worked.

How do we interpret Helene Berg's intransigent refusal to have *Lulu* published or presented as a finished opera? Was it revenge at having found out that she was a displaced muse, or was it simple distaste for the work? Whatever, it was, there was a final emotional truth for Alban Berg, well outside of the realms of his marriage and within the glories and innovations of his music. Alban Berg represented the limitless future of German music. His death at age fifty can only be seen as a senseless tragedy.

June 2001

"Dallas" auf Deutsch

I F THE TENOR of the vast abundance of books about
the works of Richard Wagner is indicative of anything, it is that it is impossible to approach the man
and his work with a light heart. His operas impose on
any listener a profound seriousness along with a sense
of awed disbelief that all of this could have been the
product of a single mind (and this simple declaration
concerning Wagner's operas does not even register his
multifaceted activities outside of the realm of music—
as critic and theoretician of the arts, politician, theater
designer, and all-around maverick).

Wagner himself would surely consider this earnest
critical attention richly deserved—he was more than
tolerant of disciples and even sycophants. Yet his wild
personality has long since disappeared into the depths
of scholarly adulation. The diaries of his second wife,
Cosima Liszt Wagner, first published in 1976 after
many vicissitudes, reveal a breezy and nonchalant
man, of whose antics she disapproved. The diaries
show a doting father who clambered up trees with his
children, loved games and parlor theater, and seems

an untrammeled spirit given to elaborate pranks and dreadful puns, as well as a voracious reader of Western literature from Homer on.

The outlines of Wagner's life and times were firmly established by Ernest Newman in his four-volume *Life of Richard Wagner* (1933–1947), a work that has been only partially supplanted by the recent one-volume treatments of Robert W. Gutman (1968), Martin Gregor-Dellin (1983), and Barry Millington (1999). Inevitably, given the recent course of cultural criticism, certain aspects of Wagner have lately been intensely scrutinized: for instance, his notorious anti-Semitism—see *Richard Wagner and the Anti-Semitic Imagination* by Marc A. Weiner (1995)—or the sexual orientations of his operatic characters—see *Wagner Androgyne* by Jean-Jacques Nattiez (1993). And even more inevitably, given the ongoing debasement of our culture, we now have such productions as the EMI CD entitled *Wagner for Dummies* or, on a more intelligent and detailed level, William Berger's book *Wagner Without Fear: Learning to Love—and Even Enjoy—Opera's Most Demanding Genius* (1998). The various works about Wagner by the Metropolitan Opera broadcasts' intermission star M. Owen Lee—most recently his *Wagner: The Terrible Man and His Truthful Art* (1999)—are sound and well-written.

Wagner's legacy would have been far more complex than most composers' even if he had not designed and built his own festival opera house (plus a home for himself and his family) in the small Franconian town of Bayreuth. The generally received opinion of music lovers is that this is madness in the form of an opera house—for instance, Mr. Frederic Spotts, author of a highly engaging history of the Bayreuth festival, noted that "To compose a fifteen-hour opera, construct a theatre solely for its performance and invite the world to attend was derided by some as vanity to the point of insanity." In 1872 a Munich analyst published a study of Wagner's personality concluding that he was "suffering from 'chronic megalomania, paranoia, ambiguous ideas and moral derangement.'" But there were plenty of fervid advocates who saw Wagner as a combination of the talents of Aeschylus, Shakespeare, and Beethoven, and moreover as an incarnation of the heroic Teutonic spirit, a musical nationalist representing the newly united Germany.

Wagner broke all the rules as he designed his ideal theater and created the incomparable acoustics at Bayreuth: singers are heard with bell-like clarity no matter what is going on in the orchestra. The Festspielhaus was envisioned as a temporary structure, however, thrown together as a prototype for a more permanent edifice. "Flimsy" is the only word for it, a carpenter's dream made entirely of pine, fir, and maple. The only twentieth-century alteration was the substitution in the 1950s of steel girders to take the place of a few perilously rotten beams. The auditorium resembles a descending Greek amphitheater and seats just under two-thousand. There is no carpet along the aisles, just bare wood. Both orchestra and conductor are invisible, hidden by an enormous hooded shell to prevent light from entering the auditorium and to

throw the sound back into the gigantic double pros-
cenium stage so that it first mixes with the singers,
bounces off the back wall, and only then reaches the
audience.

The orchestra pit consists of nine descending
straight rows of musicians, more than half of whom
must play at the lowest levels of the pit under the
stage. The first violins are placed to the right of the
conductor, the cellos and basses interspersed throughout the strings for a greater blend. The orchestra
sounds muffled in the house, intentionally subordinate
to the singers. And there are almost insurmountable
difficulties in coordination between pit and stage—
many musicians can't see the conductor, and others
can't hear any singing. The singers see only the violins
and the conductor. (These days, video monitors are an
invaluable aid.) The sound bounces around the
theater so that one cannot point to the source,
probably due to the fact that the space underneath the
thirty rows of seats is an empty wedge of air, and the
wall columns are hollow. One last oddity: the ceiling
is made of painted stretched sailcloth. Though most
performances take place in July and August, air con-
ditioning was and is unthinkable. The silence and
concentration of the audience at Bayreuth has always
been extraordinary—the "Bayreuth hush" really does
exist—and this is precisely what Wagner wanted, no
more of the unending chitchat in the boxes as at La
Scala or Charles Garnier's Paris Opera. As Mark
Twain dolefully noted in 1891, "You seem to sit with
the dead in the gloom of a tomb."

After Wagner's death in Venice on February 13, 1883, the very existence of the festival was imperiled. Wagner left no will, and a considerable sector of nationalistic Wagnerians considered the widow Cosima unfit to carry on; she wasn't "German" at all, but of Hungarian and French parentage. But with an indomitable will and intimate knowledge of Wagnerian musical and theatrical ideals, she governed the festival with an iron fist until 1906, when she handed the direction over to her son Siegfried. He was thirty-seven years old, a not untalented composer himself and a clever producer, who directed the fortunes of Bayreuth through the dark days of the Great War and the subsequent revival in 1924. But he died in 1930, just four months after his mother Cosima. This is the date from which to start a recounting of what some German wags, addicted to reruns of old American television serials, describe as "*Dallas* auf Deutsch," the unseemly and savage story of the Wagner family's management of the Bayreuth Festival.

Siegfried, Richard and Cosima's only son, had been an ebullient bachelor, continually postponing the duties of marriage and the fathering of children suitable to continue the Wagnerian tradition. What's more, he led an openly gay life, often travelling with young English gentlemen and passing off the frequent blackmail attempts to the festival treasurer, an adept at resolving these matters. Cosima was kept unaware. In 1915, the constant pressure from his mother for more fruitful domestic arrangements finally had its effect. Siegfried, aged forty-six, married the seventeen-year-old English orphan Winifred Williams, who at that time was under the guardianship of the Klindworth family, esteemed visitors at Bayreuth for many years. Four children were born: Wieland (1917), Friedelind (1918), Wolfgang (1919), and Verena (1920). The pattern established by Cosima was about to be repeated—an outsider was to invade, take over, and finally dominate Bayreuth. After Siegfried's sudden death in 1930, Winifred took over the festival and carried on until the Allied de-Nazification proceedings wrested control from her hands. Still it remained in the family with the two brothers firmly in charge when the festival reopened in 1951. It should be noted that Siegfried, liberal and free of prejudice, handed the festival over to all of his children in his will, but in the confusion following World War II, the two sons conspired with Winifred to deny the daughters any role.

I had an embarrassing but, in the end, happy en-counter with Friedelind Wagner, one of Siegfried's daughters, during a brief visit to Bayreuth in June 1962. At that time, I was unencumbered by any knowledge of the recent Wagner generations and the ongoing conflicts between the three elements of the struggle—mother, daughters, and sons. The owner of the pension where I was lodged told me that, al-though the festival had not formally begun its per-formances, I might be able to attend an afternoon re-hearsal—*Tannhäuser*, as it happened, conducted by the young Wolfgang Sawallisch. This affable lady in-formed me that, since I was an American, I should approach the Wagner grandchild who was in charge of "*die Amerikaner*," Frau Friedelind Wagner. She gave me Friedelind's address. I composed what must have been a highly garbled and ungrammatical letter in German, hoping that I might be accorded a pass to a rehearsal the next day. Having hand-delivered the letter, I was informed back at the pension that Frau Wagner would see me at ten the next morning.

At the appointed hour, Friedelind Wagner, with her unmistakable Wagnerian visage, descended the stairs with *The New Yorker*, *The Atlantic Monthly*, and *The International Herald Tribune* under her arm. With the most disarming of accents, she said to me in pure Brooklynese, "Ya know, I don't know why you wrote that letter to me in German. I've been living in Brooklyn since 1940." Years later, having finally found a copy of her stunning memoir, *Heritage of Fire* (1945), I discovered that she had always been considered the black sheep of the family, a valiant anti-Nazi who finally left Bayreuth because of her outspoken criticism of its Hitlerization. Indeed, as the last harrowing pages of that memoir demonstrate, her mother Winifred warned her in no uncertain terms: "You must stop talking, and if these measures fail the order will be given; you will be destroyed and exterminated [*austilgen und ausrotten*] at the first opportunity."

With the aid of Arturo Toscanini, who had shown great sympathy to her over the years, she escaped, made her way to Buenos Aires, and later arrived at La Guardia with Mr. and Mrs. Toscanini in 1940, applying for American citizenship. For many of the war years when things were really desperate, she earned her living by waiting on tables at Schrafft's. Needless to say, her postwar years as a visitor and sometime leader of master classes at Bayreuth were fraught with difficulty. Her mother never forgave her daughter, a "traitor to the fatherland," and her two brothers barely acknowledged her presence. In any case she was the motherly sponsor of many American singers after the war. John Rockwell's obituary in *The New York Times* of May 8, 1991 speaks of Friedelind's "gypsylike odyssey as she fruitlessly attempted to find support for her dream of a theatrical academy." Thwarted both in New York and at Bayreuth, she ordered that her ashes be scattered near her home in Lucerne. Among the Friedelind Wagner papers at the Fales Library of New York University, there is a glossy photograph of mother and daughter, more or less smiling at each other, obviously at a moment of uneasy truce. It is dated Bayreuth, 1966, one year before Friedelind was ordered to cease her summer master classes. It is signed by both mother and daughter. The mother must have signed first, since the daughter has added a sardonic comment. It reads: "To Tom [a New York friend], Lo! It's love from this summer's living monster. Friedelind." Obviously, the reference is to mother Winifred.

One of the recent witnesses to this ongoing family saga is Wieland's daughter, Nike Wagner. Ms. Wagner has recently published an overview of the past and present battles for succession at Bayreuth: *The Wag-*

ners: The Dramas of a Musical Dynasty.* It is not for nothing that Nike Wagner earned a doctorate at Northwestern University, producing a dissertation on Karl Kraus guided by the eminent scholar Erich Heller. In the first half of the book, Ms. Wagner presents us with essays on the operas and a many-layered history of their presentation. She is especially vivid in describing Wieland's "house cleaning" (*Entrümpelung*) after the war—sets for *Die Meistersinger*, for instance, without half-timbered houses, no cobbler's pegs, no grandiose processions of the craft guilds, no nationalistic paeans to "Holy German Art." His *Tristan und Isolde* and *Parsifal* were equally shocking and refreshing, and incited endless controversy between traditionalists and innovators.

She is also highly original in her speculations on the matter of incest in *Der Ring des Nibelungen* and on the influence of Otto Weininger's *Sex and Character* (1903) in the ongoing reinterpretation of sexuality and misogyny in *Parsifal*. This section of the book is a vivid and detailed defense of her father's work at Bayreuth from 1951 until his premature death in 1966. Wieland's revolutionary stagecraft completely broke with the theatrical ideologies of the past, above all by the substitution of the economy of means for the kitschy spectacles so dear to Hitler's taste. If there is a hovering, heroic figure in Nike's book, it is surely her aunt Friedelind, who receives this considerable accolade:

---

* *The Wagners: The Dramas of a Musical Dynasty*, by Nike Wagner (Princeton University Press).

Her early experience of alienation from Wahnfried [the family home at Bayreuth] and from the "primal horde of the family" were undoubtedly painful for her; at the same time, though, they gave her the detachment which later enabled her to see political affairs in a clearer light than the rest of the family.

Among so many other strands of family history here, Nike's analysis of the self-justification of Winifred Williams Wagner after the war stands out. She uses both the de-Nazification trial proceedings and the transcript of Hans-Jürgen Syberberg's five-and-one-half hour filmed interview with Winifred, one sentence from which is more than sufficient: "If Hitler came in the door today, for example, I would be just as pleased and happy as ever to see him and to have him here, and the dark side of him, I know that it exists but for me it does not exist because I do not know that side." Nike's analysis of her grandmother's silence, of what is unspoken, and of the vigorous compartmentalization of her version of Hitler and everyone else's amounts to a devastating examination of verbal tics and habits. In Nike's words, "An immaculate self-portrait is shown to be a gigantic edifice of lies."

The struggle and battle since infancy between father and uncle—between Wieland and Wolfgang—understandably occupy the psychic center of the book. This is at times unbearably painful to read, since the surviving (and supremely less talented) brother has been governing the fortunes of the festival since Wieland's death in 1966. Wagner's last grandson, Wolfgang, is now eighty-two years old and showing no signs of human frailty. In fact, he is said to be signing up singers and conductors for the 2008 season. Simply put, Nike gives us a portrait of the vengeful brother carefully carrying out a fratricidal operation against Wieland's innovations. Wolfgang's rage probably emerged in the Thirties, when the "artist" and older Wagner grandson (Wieland) was exempted by Hitler from military service—the plodding Wolfgang, more adept at administration than anything else, was badly wounded on the Eastern front. Wolfgang's behavior toward and treatment of Wieland's family and the legacy of his historic productions only proves the point, a "getting even" that lasts to this day.

Difficult as it is to envision, the direction of the Bayreuth Festival will ultimately change hands. In 1973, a foundation was set up with the complete cooperation of the family, the province, and the federal government. This entity will choose the next director. (There are twenty-four votes on the nominating commission, of which the family has only five.) Many candidates are already jockeying for position, and it is clear that the present volume is Nike Wagner's presentation of her credentials for the directorship. Indeed, the final chapter is entitled "1990–2000, The Battle for Succession," and on page 310 we see a paragraph beginning with "My plan for the restructuring of the Festival . . ." All sympathetic readers can only wish her luck. At this writing, however, Nike's aspirations may have already come to naught. In the Spring of 2001, the Wagner Foundation tried to force the resignation of Wolfgang Wagner in favor of his daughter, Eva Wagner-Pasquier, who has had considerable administrative experience at Covent Garden, the Bastille Opera, and the Metropolitan Opera. It must be kept in mind that the foundation has total power over the functioning of the house (the Wagner family no longer has any say except through their votes in the foundation) and the whole of Richard Wagner's Bayreuth is now a semi-public property, supported by government funds. Wolfgang, who insists that he has a lifetime contract, rejected the nomination of his daughter Eva, totally estranged as they are, and instead volunteered to step down in favor of his second wife, Gudrun, who would hold the post until their daughter Katharina attains her majority. This solution was rejected out of hand by the foundation.

Knowing the history of the "luxuriant dysfunctionality" typical of the family, it comes as no surprise that Eva informed *The Financial Times* that "My father has become a little dictator" and turned down the foundation's nomination. Nasty rhetoric is coming from all quarters. The exasperated Bavarian Minister for Culture, Hans Zehetmair, has described Wolfgang as "Rumpelstiltskin" and "an old goat" and has threatened to cancel all contracts "if a new generation is not allowed to take up the reins." At this summer's performances, a chorus of boos greeted Juergen Flimm's *Ring*, Placido Domingo resigned in a huff, and the Brünnhilde, Gabriele Schnaut, pulled out. A star conductor, Giuseppe Sinopoli, died unexpectedly, replaced by the competent Adam Fischer. Not without precedent, Bayreuth is in a crisis.

Wolfgang threatens legal action to retain his post, and he has many cards left to play. *The Guardian* reports that the young German director Christoph Schlingensief, who recently cast a group of neo-Nazis in a production of *Hamlet*, has a future at Bayreuth, as does the highly nationalistic young conductor Christian Thielemann. It has been noted that since a new *Ring* is now in the works for 2006, a new director might not affect things in any substantial fashion until 2013.

Fifty thousand tickets are issued each season, and the waiting list indicates that, if you apply without further delay, tickets are available for the Summer of 2008.

December 2001

"Der Rosenkavalier"

I T WAS QUITE a shock to take down from my library shelf Joseph Kerman's esteemed study *Opera as Drama* (1956) and be reminded that an opera I love did not pass muster. For Kerman, Richard Strauss's *Der Rosenkavalier* consists of "four finicky hours of leitmotives, modulations, and program-musical wit." He writes that "the opening tableau is already so enervated in sentiment that the relationship between Octavian and the Marschallin seems as unappetizing as their affectionate nicknames" and that "the scene of the presentation of the rose has all the solidity of a fifty-cent valentine." Moreover, Kerman concludes, "no one who has understood *The Marriage of Figaro* could ever have taken *Der Rosenkavalier* seriously, unless it was Strauss and Hofmannsthal, and even that is not certain."

Strange—all throughout 1999, the fiftieth anniversary year of the death of Richard Strauss, there has been a fulsome celebration of his life and work with the publication in English of no less than *four* full length studies, not to mention the recent reissue of Kurt Wilhelm's richly illustrated study, *Richard Strauss: An Intimate Portrait* (Thames & Hudson).* Pace Kerman, *Der Rosenkavalier* occupies an important place in all four of these recently published scholarly examinations, and this constant and seemingly ever increasing interest was confirmed and amplified by a brilliant revival/restoration at the Metropolitan Opera this winter of Nathaniel Merrill's thirty-year-old staging, brushed up and briskly conducted by James Levine. An encore broadcast on PBS of the 1982 version of this same production, featuring Kiri Te Kanawa, Tatiana Troyanos, Judith Blegen, and Luciano Pavarotti, is scheduled to be seen on March 22 of this year. Last but not at all least, the Met is issuing (for a $150 donation) a CD set of a 1951 performance of the opera, featuring Eleanor Steber, Jarmila Novotná, and Erna Berger, all under the imperious baton of Fritz Reiner.

The Met's six performances of an apparently uncut *Der Rosenkavalier* (going from 7:30 P.M. to 12:05 A.M., counting the two intermissions), with a thankfully unchanging cast and with the added public benefit of a matinee broadcast on Saturday, January 29, gave evidence of scrupulous preparation and sensitive casting. The three principal female roles are crucial—in these performances, the trio consisted of

---

* *Richard Strauss*, by Tim Ashley (Phaidon Press). *Richard Strauss*, by Matthew Boyden (Northeastern University Press). *Richard Strauss: Man, Musician, Enigma*, by Michael Kennedy (Cambridge University Press). *The Life of Richard Strauss*, by Bryan Gilliam (Cambridge University Press).

88

mezzo Susan Graham as Octavian, soprano Renée Fleming as the Marschallin, and high soprano (Strauss's term) Heidi Grant Murphy as Sophie. It is a commonplace in Strauss criticism that he had a "love affair" with women's voices. Nothing could be more obvious, if we take into account the prominent and exacting demands for the voice in such works as *Salome* (1905), *Elektra* (1909), *Der Rosenkavalier* (1911), on down to the autumnal eloquence of *Capriccio* (1942) and of course the sublime *Four Last Songs* (1948). After all, Strauss's wife, the formidable soprano Pauline de Ahna, was a renowned performer in her time. She sang at Bayreuth at the invitation of Cosima Wagner, and accompanied Strauss in a concert tour of the United States in 1904, giving some thirty-five song recitals. Although she left behind no recordings and stopped performing after the American tour, we have some idea of what she sounded like. The curmudgeonly critic Eduard Hanslick, the bane of Wagner's existence, reviewed a Vienna recital of Pauline de Ahna, accompanied by her husband. Hanslick exclaimed, "Frau de Ahna's excellently trained, rich, sweet soprano did our hearts good! We may surely call her his better and more beautiful half." We may rightfully presume that there is a musical agenda behind Hanslick's praise. Just prior to Frau Strauss's recital, he had once again displayed his anti-Wagnerian stance by drubbing her husband's tone poem *Ein Heldenleben* on the occasion of its Vienna premiere.

The particular voice timbre preferred by Strauss,

both "rich" and "sweet," can be heard, for instance, in the 1933 abridged recording of *Der Rosenkavalier*, featuring Maria Olczewska as Octavian, Lotte Lehmann as the Marschallin, and the Sophie of Elisabeth Schumann. It was no surprise that Strauss should describe Lotte Lehmann as "the ideal interpreter of my operas." Closer to our times, another kind of preferred timbre can be heard in the voice of Ljuba Welitsch, the Bulgarian soprano whom Strauss had personally coached just before a performance of *Salome* at the Vienna State Opera in 1944. Five years later, in 1949, Welitsch made a stunning monophonic recording of the final scene from *Salome*, accompanied by Fritz Reiner and the Metropolitan Opera Orchestra—a performance that still occupies a special place in the now wildly abundant Strauss discography. Even closer to our times are such singers as Hilde Gueden, Sena Jurinac, Maria Reining, Elisabeth Schwarzkopf, Lisa della Casa, and Teresa Stich-Randall, naming only six singers and thus unfairly excluding so many other distinguished Marschallins, Octavians, and Sophies from the past three decades.

Each individual voice here mentioned might collectively give us the ideal composite Strauss soprano or mezzo. How to describe what he wanted? In spite of the sometimes hypertrophic orchestral accompaniment supporting his sopranos and mezzos during this period of Strauss's compositions, it can be said that Strauss was always searching for something different from a Wagnerian singer, typified by the opulence and majesty we now associate with Kirsten Flagstad and, more recently, Birgit Nilsson. Again and again, scholars find the composer begging for a relatively light, silvery voice—not thin, but penetrating and able to cut through the rich orchestral fabric. For instance, he wanted, paradoxically, a light and capricious singer for his ideal Salome, with a "childish charm" and a "latent sensuality," in the words of Michael Kennedy.

In this regard, the young Herbert von Karajan recalled that Strauss once complained to him: "Nowadays all the heavy voices are singing *Salome*. It's all gone out of control. I *don't* want this!" In this sense, Welitsch was perfect, giving out a sense of girlish passion—with touches of the sinister—hovering over a purposefully turgid and declamatory orchestral web. This kind of voice is also particularly suited to the operas of Strauss's beloved idol Mozart, at odds with the voices needed for the operas of Strauss's youthful infatuation, Wagner. It must always be kept in mind that Strauss, as conductor and sometime head of the opera houses in Berlin and Vienna in his maturity, was primarily responsible for the return of Mozart's *Così fan tutte* to the European opera house repertory, the work having been relegated to oblivion by misguided romantic ideas about Mozart as the composer of a powdered rococo trifle.

Keeping in mind the relevance still of Strauss's sonic ideal, the trio of singers heard at the Met's first performance of the season and the matinee broadcast were all nicely bright in tone with the always appropriate metallic edge during dialogue and ensembles. This listener had the distinct impression that

Susan Graham as Octavian gave the most forceful characterization within the trio, while Renée Fleming was a distanced, pure-toned, and occasionally inaudible Marschallin of slightly less than majestic carriage in the last act. The difficult role of Sophie, a vapid ninny if there ever was one, had a fine interpreter in Heidi Grant Murphy; her hard tone complemented the more rounded timbres of the other two.

As for the Ochs von Lerchenau of Franz Hawlata, it was good to see a baron of less than Falstaffian girth. Nevertheless, there were slapstick touches that really went beyond the pale. Long ago, having learned some hard lessons from witnessing innumerable productions of the opera, Strauss himself warned both singers and directors that

> most basses have presented [Ochs] as a disgusting vulgar monster with a repellent mask and proletarian manners. . . . This is quite wrong: Ochs must be a rustic beau of thirty-five, who is after all a member of the gentry, if somewhat countrified.

The impression given at the Met was that the singer had fallen into coarseness, both musical and visual; there was no sense of ironic pomp or the comic deflation that the role suggests.

The orchestra under Maestro Levine cannot be sufficiently praised, above all in the deft realization of the "Introduction and Pantomime" music at the beginning of Act III, marked to be played "as fast as possible." I am reminded of rule number nine of

Strauss's not-quite-to-be-taken-seriously *Ten Golden Rules for the Album of a Young Conductor*: "When you think you have reached the limits of *prestissimo*, double the pace." Levine and the orchestra did just that. He is a master of this complex score, and the performance was nothing if not efficient, though it could hardly be said to exude charm and *gemütlichkeit* at all times.

Performance styles change. For instance, to what extent can we take as authoritative a particular recording that a composer such as Strauss has made of one of his works? In an interview with Paul Myers of the then Columbia Records, George Szell remembered Strauss's conductorial performances as "very often perfunctory. He might be aglow and aflame directing *Così fan tutte*, *Tristan und Isolde*, *Die Walküre*, or *Fidelio*, but intensely *boring* with *Der Rosenkavalier* or *Salome*. It would seem that the music had lost interest for him the moment he had finished with it."

This impression is further confirmed by available film excerpts of Strauss conducting portions of *Der Rosenkavalier*. They are remarkably uninflected and unemphatic. The conductor Fritz Busch noted that "Nothing annoyed [Strauss] more than when conductors wallowed in his lyrical outpourings." If anything characterizes contemporary interpretations of *Der Rosenkavalier* such as Levine's or, say, Bernstein's and Solti's, it is that they have much more heft and gravity than those produced during Strauss's lifetime. They also tend to dawdle, as Strauss never did. He just wanted to get back into the wings to continue his favorite card game, "Skat." In this sense, Robert Heger's blithe, fluent conducting of the abridged 1933 *Der Rosenkavalier* stands either as an admirable performance ideal or one that, by our standards today, is insufficiently pointed, without springy accents.

One last and not at all minor detail: Strauss's ideal Ochs von Lerchenau, Richard Mayr (who was prevented from singing in the 1911 premiere because of contractual obligations), finally recorded his stupendous reading of the role in this 1933 recording. You only have to see a few minutes of the *Rosenkavalier* video filmed at Salzburg in 1962 under Herbert von Karajan, and featuring one of Mayr's heirs apparent, Otto Edelmann, in the role of Ochs, to realize how the projection of porcine gallantry can work on the stage without any heavy burlesque. This elusive touch in a performer is what Alan Rich called the "tastefully controlled low comedy of Edelmann's Ochs." As the Marschallin so clearly states at the end of Act I, "Leicht muss man sein, mit leichtem Herzen und leichten Händen" ("One must take it lightly, with light heart and light hands").

Our four Strauss scholars seem to agree that, after the blaring dissonances of *Elektra*, which certified Strauss as an avant-gardist, both librettist and composer enthusiastically declared a "time out" to indulge in an exercise of what might be called the anachronistic imagination. As one critic put it, Strauss "had had enough of murder and perversion." It was necessary to follow *Elektra* with a "Mozart" opera, a "psychological comedy with both mischievous and sweet characters, and, like a Beaumarchais play, containing round misunderstandings, love's complications, and disguises in which nobody recognizes anybody," as George R. Marek said. It must have been irresistible for both Hofmannsthal and Strauss to go back to an imagined time where, at the proper distance, courtly punctilio was observed in the text, if not in the music. The elaborate polyphony, occasional orchestral surfeit, and what Strauss himself admitted were "longueurs"—plus the waltzes outrageously inappropriate for an eighteenth-century setting—all these matters were grave problems for a few observers, in spite of the wholesale acclaim.

Strauss recognized his tendency to varnish his music. As Norman del Mar noted in his definitive three-volume study of Strauss's music,

> [An] absolute mastery of technique had, of course, its own special dangers. He could scarcely look at a page of score without new counterpoints suggesting themselves instantly to him, a "verdammte Begabung," as he described it, a damned gift which he was well aware prompted him often to overfill his scores.

Along the same lines, Thomas Mann wrote an enraged letter of sympathy to Hofmannsthal after the premiere. Mann was inconsolable:

> What in God's name do you really feel about the way Strauss has loaded and stretched your airy structure?

> A charming joke weighed down by four hours of din!
> . . . Where is Vienna, where is the eighteenth century
> in this music? Hardly in the waltzes. They are
> anachronistic, and put the stamp of operetta on the
> entire work. . . . Not a word can be heard.

It should be said that the conductor at the 1911
premiere, Ernst von Schuch, was renowned for
drowning out his singers. At the Met, the text came
across with distinct enunciation, except for the moments when one of the singers had to race through a
part as written by Strauss. The result is a Straussian
"gabble," something of which he was very aware, and
which is impossible to understand, no matter what
language the opera might be sung in. As Strauss so
ruefully admitted in his recollections of the first performances of the opera, "The evening was a little long
drawn out, since, in my enthusiasm, I had composed
the whole of the somewhat talkative text without alteration, although even the author had expected me to
make cuts."

Still, unlike most opera librettos, Hofmannsthal's
deserves close scrutiny beforehand. As Mr. Gilliam
perceptively notes in his straightforward biography of
Strauss, the opera is

> about time and transformation on multiple levels. . . .
> Octavian himself takes on various transformations, as
> the Marschallin's adolescent lover, as her chamber-
> maid, as a rose cavalier, and—by the end—as a wiser
> young man. . . . To Hofmannsthal, the miracle of life

is that an old love can die, while a new one can arise in its ashes.

Moreover, there is more in the way of social commentary than is generally recognized. Hofmannsthal knew all about acquired nobility and sudden social ascension. As Ilse Barea tells the story in her still useful book on Vienna, the founder of the Hofmannsthal fortune centuries back, a silk merchant from Prague, came to Vienna and, once ennobled by the court, endearingly chose for his coat of arms a mulberry leaf (symbol of the silk industry) for one field of the escutcheon, and the tablets of the Mosaic law for the other. This man's son married an Italian woman and converted to Catholicism. Further on down the genealogical line, Hugo von Hofmannsthal grew up as a Catholic, but was conscious of his Jewish ancestry: *arrivisme* was in the air. Theodor W. Adorno, in his scrutiny of the correspondence between Stefan George and Hofmannsthal, gave an acid portrait of the ambitious pretensions of the young Hofmannsthal:

> It is the diligent cosmopolitanism of the young gentleman of good family, the model which Hofmannsthal later used in stylizing his own past, a legend from the very first. His is the laxity of one who identifies with the aristocracy, or at least with that kind of upper-class society which shares most of its interests and knows its way around.

In his time, Hofmannsthal was able to observe the

turn-of-the-century equivalents of a few wistful Marschallins of a certain age, accompanied by their passionate Italianate loves such as Octavian Rofrano. Also within his salon scrutiny were such types as the ambitious Faninal and his newly eligible daughter Sophie, she just out of the convent (as was the Marschallin before her arranged marriage a few decades before). In the opera, all of the foregoing characters are soon to be put to the test by the intrusion of the rough-hewn blueblood Ochs von Lerchenau, intent as he is of making use of his decrepit title to liquidate some long-standing debts by means of a suitable marriage to Sophie. In turn, pater Faninal, recently enriched as a purveyor to the troops in Flanders and possessor of twelve rentable houses, needs Ochs for his ascension in Viennese society just as much as Ochs needs financial relief. Social ambitions collude with the financial need of a wasted aristocracy. The same interaction between arrivistes and proud bluebloods occurs in Lampedusa's *The Leopard*.

Strauss himself, the son of the horn player Franz Strauss (who had risen in society by marrying the heiress of a Munich brewery), contracted marriage with the imperious daughter of an army general. Pauline de Ahna never permitted her composer-husband to forget his relative social inferiority within the echelons of Bavarian society. By most accounts (those of Alma and Gustav Mahler, Pauline Dehmel, and Lotte Lehmann), it was a bizarre marriage. Lehmann was the most devastating witness: Frau Strauss called him a peasant and their marriage a *mésalliance*; she could have had a dashing hussar, and his music couldn't compare with that of Massenet. Richard refused to be ruffled: "'Believe me, Lotte,' he said to me the day I was leaving, 'the whole world's admiration interests me a great deal less than a single one of Pauline's fits of rage.'" It is true that he prided himself in playing out the role of Bavarian bumpkin. In this regard, Hofmannsthal's description of Strauss in a letter to a friend sounds strangely like the Marschallin in her confrontations with Ochs:

> [Strauss] is such an incredibly unrefined person, he has such a frightful bent toward triviality and kitsch . . . an extraordinarily mixed character, but vulgarity rises in him as easily as groundwater.

The baffling marriage takes up a considerable amount of space in these four studies of Strauss; other points in common are the nature of his changing collaborations with Hofmannsthal up until the latter's tragic death in 1929; the mixed fortunes of Strauss's post-Hofmannsthal collaborations with Stefan Zweig, Josef Gregor, and Clemens Krauss; his ongoing interest in lieder composition and orchestral works, culminating in the final instrumental masterpiece, the *Metamorphosen* for twenty-three solo strings, composed in 1944–1945.

If any major distinctions are to be made among these four books on Strauss, they lie in the varying interpretations and emphases on the relationship of

Strauss to the Nazis. It is notoriously well known that the composer carried out a cynical dalliance with the movement known as National Socialism: he occupied official posts in their cultural ministry, was photographed effusively shaking hands with Goebbels, and wrote a fawning letter to Hitler. It is less well known that his only son Franz had married a woman of part-Jewish ancestry, that the couple was constantly threatened with arrest and deportation (and in fact was arrested for a short time), that Strauss's grandchildren wore the yellow star of David to school in Garmisch, thereby inciting the local toughs against them and the whole family, in spite of their eminence. Foolishly thinking, as did Wilhelm Furtwängler, that an accommodation with the regime was possible in the Thirties, Strauss got his comeuppance in the early Forties. By then, he was formally declared non grata, and indeed underwent a confrontational excoriation personally delivered by Goebbels: "Stop all your claptrap about the importance of serious music, once and for all. Tomorrow's art is different from yesterday's. You, Herr Strauss, belong to yesterday!"

All four Strauss scholars try to be fair each in their own way with this ignominious twelve-year-long episode. Michael Kennedy is the most judicious and balanced, bordering on the apologetic. Mr. Ashley sees Strauss as flailing between two extremes: "On occasion, he acted out of self-interest, or, even worse, personal spite; there were other times when he was, without question, deliberately persecuted and emotionally blackmailed." Matthew Boyden's study, especially rich on the cultural background of Strauss's youth and adolescence, contains the most unrelentingly negative portrait of Strauss as a man. It must be said that the facts do not have to be at all twisted by any observer to make the man Strauss into a cold, calculating machine for luxuriant musical composition. As Boyden sourly notes,

> the unease to which he was prone during his last four years does point towards the existence of a conscience, but it might just as easily be argued that he was fearful for the future of his music in a world hateful to anyone and anything connected with Hitler's Reich.

As for the other three studies: Kennedy's is the most encyclopedic, while Ashley and Gilliam work with the same material in a more elegant and selective manner.

None of these academic studies can answer what Fritz Busch called in 1949

> the puzzle of Strauss, who in spite of his marvellous talents is not really penetrated and possessed by them like other great artists but, in fact, simply wears them like a suit of clothes which can be taken off at will—this puzzle neither I nor anyone else has yet succeeded in solving.

Strauss himself, in an uncommonly blunt moment of self-assessment, told Stefan Zweig in 1934 that

DIVERSIONS AND ANIMADVERSIONS

what suits me best, South German bourgeois that I am, are sentimental jobs; but such bull's eyes as the *Arabella* duet and the *Der Rosenkavalier* trio don't happen every day. Must one become seventy years old to recognize that one's greatest strength lies in creating kitsch?

Not at all in his dotage, can the composer himself have been that far wrong?

March 2000

Toscanini in His Letters

To the waning numbers of music lovers who have a clear memory of a live or even a recorded performance conducted by Arturo Toscanini (1867–1957), it must be galling to note how the grandeur of his achievement is gradually diminishing, principally among the two or three most recent generations of musicians and music lovers. The testimony from past audiences on particular live performances of Toscanini heard, let's say, at La Scala, Bayreuth, Vienna, or Salzburg before the war attests to the stunning impact of this conductor on musicians and audiences alike. Yet this history must come from written reports and interviews; whatever primitive recordings of such performances exist are still not available to the general public.

As for the recordings that are available, I note that many younger listeners just can't bear even to listen to a monophonic recording made by Toscanini and his heroic NBC Symphony, let alone a reissue made from old 78s from his splendid epoch with the New York Philharmonic. For them, it is just too hard on the ear—they only go for the digital recording, or stereo-phonic at the very least.

Something else is on the wane—the fanatic adulation of certain music lovers and critics alleging the superiority of Toscanini's performances over all others. I myself can attest to this fervor. Living in Cambridge, Massachusetts in the mid-1960s, I invited a teaching colleague from Wellesley College to supper, and he brought along the distinguished musical critic B. H. Haggin, whose trenchant reviews of recent recordings were a mainstay of the back pages of *The Yale Review* at that time. I was blissfully unaware that he was a major advocate and friend of Toscanini, and he was in the process of preparing his book *The Toscanini Musicians Knew*, a compilation of testimonies from musicians from both the New York Philharmonic and the NBC Symphony, later published in 1967. What's worse, I had not yet read his *Conversations With Toscanini*, which had been published in 1959. Prior to the pasta, I made what was to be the fatal error of the evening, playing the opening bars of the Beethoven Fourth Symphony as recorded during the war by Wilhelm Furtwängler directing the Berlin Philharmonic—a languorous interpretation, it must be said, above all in the opening adagio. The explosion of wrath from my guest almost ruined the evening. I should have known—I was later to confirm on many occasions Haggin's searing contempt for almost any wielder of the baton other than Toscanini.

HARVEY SACHS, the editor of the present compilation

of Toscanini letters is also a fervent admirer of Toscanini. He is the author of a balanced and authoritative biography, *Toscanini* (1978), along with a collection of essays on various aspects of the Toscanini legacy, *Reflections on Toscanini* (1991). At the same time, he has a broad comprehension of the achievements of other conductors, and is not at all the fanatic that he might have been, given his dedication to the subject. His biography is a careful appraisal of Toscanini's career. Some highlights therein include the following: a cellist under Verdi's baton for the premiere of *Otello*; conducting the first performances of *I Pagliacci* and *La Bohème* respectively; his advocacy of the then unperformed Wagner in Italy (*Götter-dämmerung*, Turin, 1895); at age 31, principal conductor of La Scala; directing the Italian premiere of *Pélleas et Mélisande* (La Scala, 1908); touring Europe with the New York Philharmonic (1930); *Missa Solemnis* and *Requiem* (Verdi) with the Vienna Philharmonic (1934, 1936); the first non-German conductor at Bayreuth (*Tristan und Isolde*, *Tannhäuser*, *Parsifal*, 1930–1933); at the Salzburg Festival in the late thirties with his peerless performances of *Fidelio*, *Falstaff*, and *Die Meistersinger*; founder and principal conductor of the NBC Symphony, 1937–1954, including a tour of South America in 1940 and a killer eight-week U.S. tour, to California and back, in 1950 (at age eighty-three).

As any Toscanini recording demonstrates, his

---

* *The Letters of Arturo Toscanini* (Alfred A. Knopf).

"energy, singlemindedness, impetuosity combined with an inflexible will, fanatical perfectionism . . . [were] among Toscanini's most remarkable characteristics" (David Cairns). As a final measure of the breadth of his inexhaustible energies and abilities, one notes the number of contemporary works the Romantic Toscanini conducted over the years—works by Stravinsky, Honegger, Shostakovich, Sibelius, Roy Harris, even Aaron Copland's *El Salón México*. Admittedly, Mahler, Schoenberg, and Berg were anathema—on one occasion after hearing a rehearsal of Berg's *Lulu* in Venice in the late Forties, Toscanini expressed his displeasure by opening the lid of a nearby piano and sitting on the keys.

In his 1978 biography, Mr. Sachs rarely attempted to make psychological insights into what drove Toscanini to such splendid artistic excesses, but there were moments when the biographer suggested that "Toscanini was not a cheerful character by nature. He flourished only when working insanely hard, and at a pitch of tension which would have destroyed any normal human being." The motive behind such furious activity, fleeing from God knows what, was not evident to the biographer in 1978, since "Toscanini's letters . . . are relatively few and uninformative." Still, even before the publication of these sensational letters in the present volume, it was evident that Toscanini was plagued by an eternal and cosmic sense of dissatisfaction, a rage against the self, along with the consciousness, in music terms, of the distance between the ideal performance he heard in his head and the ordinary music-making typical of most concerts. This is what constantly produced those epic outbursts that we can hear in some of the bootleg rehearsal recordings. Here are four of my favorite imprecations to members of the NBC Symphony, Toscanini always shouting as a musical Stentor, never talking:

"It is impossible to believe that you can be so stupid! You can't believe, no!! Corpo di Dio Santissimo! Madonna Santissima!"

"You don't know what the Italian 'andante' means?"

"Be intelligent, per Dio Santo!!"

"Open your ears!!"

In many ways, the present volume offers a more intimate view into what Arturo Toscanini always wanted to protect against any publicity—his personal demons, along with a stunning diary of the sensual and erotic life of a conductor whose adventures in this area were utterly unknown to the public at large. There was a grand precedent for all this—the intimate life of Verdi in old age. As Toscanini said, "He wrote Falstaff when he was eighty, Otello when he was seventy-four; do you think that a man of such fiber would be satisfied doing nothing but reciting the Ave Maria?" The letters moreover offer us a depth of insight into Toscanini's relations to such composers as Mahler, Strauss, and Puccini; his opinions of other conductors (mostly negative); his musical negotiations with La Scala, the Metropolitan Opera, the New York

Philharmonic, the Bayreuth Festival, the Salzburg Festival; his epic and finally triumphant feuds with German and Italian fascism; and, of course, the final apotheosis before, during, and after the war in the United States with the NBC Symphony. As Mr. Sachs is the first to admit, these letters add many levels of knowledge to the general outlines of Toscanini's achievements that he first offered to us in his Toscanini biography of 1978.

Mr. Sachs, in diligent cooperation with Toscanini's grandson Walfredo, has collected a sample of some of the most important letters brought to light since the publication of his Toscanini biography—namely, forty letters sent to one Elsa Kurzbauer, an intimate friend, that Mr. Sachs characterizes as "largely pornographic documents . . . of little musical-historical value." Then, in 1995, some one thousand letters and telegrams were bought at auction—these were sent by Toscanini to Ada Colleoni Mainardi, the wife of the cellist Enrico Mainardi. Mr. Sachs reluctantly admits that since these two sets of letters are the principal basis of this collection, these "aforementioned erotic-pornographic ravings occupy a disproportionate segment of his extant correspondence." It might be gently affirmed that no part of the female body herein remains unmentioned, untouched, or unevoked. Mrs. Toscanini, Carla de Montini, whom he married in 1897, is a ghostly and unwanted presence throughout these letters; it is a terrible thing to say, but his children from the marriage seem altogether more a nuisance than a joy.

There was a word limit imposed by the publishers, however, and the editor has "decided to restrict the ravings to a few choice examples and to concentrate instead on letters . . . [concerning] his music making and his whole persona." This he has done. Mr. Sachs insists, and I believe him, that he has not acted as a censor, but rather as an editor of an otherwise unmanageable quantity of outlandish, operatic, volcanic passion and ardor, as expressed in terms that might give pause to anyone. As Mr. Sachs diplomatically instructs us in his introduction, "these letters are reminders of the fact that overheated sexuality is often a concomitant and sometimes an important component of intense spirituality."

Amen.

Internet special, Summer 2002

Houses of Repute

DECADES AGO Sir Peter Ustinov was called upon to write an introduction to an amusing anthology about calamities that have ocurred in the major opera houses of the West—appropriately entitled *Great Operatic Disasters*. Sir Peter began with a memorable definition: "There is no art form which attempts the sublime while defying the ridiculous with quite the foolhardiness of opera." The book is full of misbehaving horses, dentures lost in the stage gloom, grotesquely misclad baritones, Rigoletto's hump gradually slipping down the hapless singer's back ("One would have thought that they *knew* something about handling hunchbacks in Paris"). And this is not even to begin to consider the quality of the singing, of which Ustinov gives us a few classifications: "Those who can sing but can't act . . . those who can act but who can no longer sing . . . those paragons who can both sing and act . . . and finally, those who can neither act nor sing, retained in harness by some humanitarian pension scheme."

It must be said that the proper execution of what

Wagner used to call the *Gesamtkunstwerk*, the bringing together of drama, song, dance, and instrumental sound, is a high-risk operation at the best of times. Even a ballet evening can go wrong for the most modest of reasons. The Associated Press recently reported that, at London's elegant Royal Opera House, Covent Garden, about two-thousand ballet fans had to be evacuated after a baked potato exploded in a backstage microwave oven and triggered the fire alarm.

Any major opera house can expect to have its history recounted, and three of the world's most important have received treatment in recent books: the Metropolitan Opera in New York; the Royal Opera House, Covent Garden (ROH); and the Kirov Opera in St. Petersburg.*

Johanna Fiedler certainly knows her way around the world of music. She is the daughter of the Boston Pops conductor Arthur Fiedler, and in her previous book, *Arthur Fiedler: Papa, the Pops, and Me*, she gave us a frank view of her irascible father, who was continually humbled by the BSO's Serge Koussevitzky. She was also the Metropolitan Opera's general press representative from 1975–1989 and had the fullest possible cooperation of archivists, critics, singers,

---

* *Molto Agitato: The Mayhem Behind the Music at the Metropolitan Opera*, by Johanna Fiedler (Doubleday).
Covent Garden: The Untold Story (Dispatches from the English Culture War, 1945–2000), by Norman Lebrecht (Northeastern University Press).
Valery Gergiev and the Kirov: A Story of Survival, by John Ardoin (Amadeus Press).

agents, board members, and, of course, the general manager Joseph Volpe and the artistic director James Levine.

Ms. Fiedler had no pretensions to writing a serious overview of the history of the Met before her arrival. After all, Irving Kolodin had produced a massive history of the institution, *The Metropolitan Opera 1883–1966: A Candid History*, of well over seven hundred pages, covering the history of the house before Lincoln Center. Hers is a personal scrutiny of the Met as she knew it. The present music director, James Levine, first appeared on the Met podium in 1971 as a young twenty-eight-year-old wunderkind. Understandably, given his achievements, he is the central figure in the latter parts of her book.

Molto Agitato is not a book about singing, but rather a story about "operatic" struggles within the Met's management and about performers facing each other and management down. In their respective battles with exasperated general managers, both Maria Callas and Kathleen Battle were to be summarily fired for behavioral excess—the lesson being that even great singers can only go so far. All sorts of other conflicts are recounted herein—between the board and general manager, between singers, between the orchestra and management, even between the orchestra and their beloved conductor: Levine has been known to wing it. "One mild complaint," Ms. Fiedler writes, "is that Jimmy sight-reads the scores at first rehearsals for operas he has never done before. After the first rehearsal for one Met premiere, he praised the orchestra. 'That was very good for a first run-through,' he said, and one of the musicians replied, under his breath, 'We could say the same to you.'" Nonetheless, the Volpe/Levine years are much celebrated here, and deservedly so. In her treatment of Maestro Levine, she is frank, but I wonder what kind of biting, untrammeled critical study might have resulted if *Molto Agitato* had not been written by an observer who is so obviously a supremely loyal former member of the Met staff.

TWO MATTERS ought to be mentioned in reference to the Met that contrast it to the other two houses under the microscope. The Met has always been funded by private generosity, beginning with the largesse of Otto Kahn, Eleanor Robson Belmont, and Cornelius Bliss, then with the ever more energetic fundraising from the Metropolitan Opera Guild and the popular Saturday afternoon broadcasts, and on to the cultivation of generous individual benefactors, such as Sybil Harrington and Alberto Vilar. Ticket prices have never been cheap, though standing room was and is a bargain. The point is that the government never enters *Molto Agitato* as a subject of concern or preoccupation, whereas, for the other two opera houses under consideration, Whitehall (after the Labour Party victory in July 1945) and Moscow (before and after the Soviet years) are essential topics. The second point is that while ballet is entirely subsidiary to operatic production at the Met, the Royal Ballet at Covent Garden and the Mariinsky/Kirov Ballet are immensely powerful presences in the scheduling and administration of both the British and Russian companies.

Not only is Covent Garden another kind of opera house, but Mr. Norman Lebrecht is quite another kind of critic. He is an outsider, an intruder into the sacred temple of classical music, a wild man, even. As a freewheeling music columnist for London's *Daily Telegraph* and the author of the much discussed *Maestro Myth* (1991) and *When the Music Stops* (1997; published in the United States under the more appropriate title *Who Killed Classical Music? Maestros, Managers, and Corporate Politics*), he can be fairly described as music criticism's only cultural guerrilla—there is no one comparable to him in the United States (see his weekly *Telegraph* articles at www.scena.org). What is more, he is the host of a weekly interactive BBC Radio 3 talk show, "Lebrecht Live," in which unprepared participants, expecting the rattling of teacups, find themselves challenged, scrutinized, and criticized, if not excoriated, in ways that poor little NPR here in the U. S. of A. can only fantasize about. Indeed, after reading anew *Who Killed Classical Music?*, I can only imagine what was left on the cutting room floor after the legal vetting. Mr. Lebrecht took on the titans of classical music management and showed how the concentration of "stars"—the "Three Tenors" being only the worst example—has crowded out even the most distinguished young talent, vocal and instrumental.

The subtitle of Mr. Lebrecht's history of the ROH— "Dispatches from the English Cultural War, 1945–

2000"—is indicative of the social breadth of his inquiry. His grand theme—the role of government in arts dissemination and the ultimate failure of such a program—starts with Churchill's stunning defeat by Labour in the summer of 1945. With its cities in ruins, a shabbily dressed populace, and food and fuel rationing that would last ten years more, Britain had won the war and lost the peace. All the more remarkable, therefore, was the intense cultural messianism advocated by the new government. It created the Arts Council, reinforced the dedication of the BBC Third Programme to music, and began the support of the Royal Opera House at Covent Garden. Much of this was due to the superhuman energies and fine political hand of John Maynard Keynes and his ballerina wife, Lydia Lopokova. In a radio address, Keynes intoned: "We look forward to a time when the theatre and the concert hall and the gallery will be a living element in everyone's upbringing." England would rise again alright, but much more enlightened from its economic Dunkirk. "The arts—the creative voice of the nation—were from now on to be a paternal concern of central government." Keynes was the first to occupy the Arts Council chair—he rescued the opera house from the dance hall that it was during the war and married ballet irrevocably to the future Royal Opera House with the help of the imperious Dame Ninette de Valois (née Edris Stannis). Keynes was followed over the years by Ernest Pooley, Sir Kenneth Clark, and most significantly, Garrett Moore, Eleventh Earl of Drogheda, who lasted from 1959–1974.

Mr. Lebrecht's 580-page inquiry asks a simple question: How could an innocent governmental subvention of £25,000 in 1945, which aided in the official re-opening of the ROH on February 20, 1946, end with the two-year closure of the house in the late Nineties for complete renovations costing some £214 million? The story, as one observer put it, is "the longest running arts farce" in the nation's history. One crucial element in all this, not noted by Mr. Lebrecht until page 494, was that donations to the arts in Britain were *not* tax deductible until the Inland Revenue law was changed in 2000. And state subsidies, while new to Britain in 1945, were and are still meager compared to those doled out in Germany. The Munich Opera House is supported by a 70 percent state subsidy, a sum inconceivable to the Exchequer no matter whether Tory or Labour resided at No. 11.

But after all this, one can still understand Mr. Lebrecht's ultimate exasperation when he notes that, because of innumerable delays over the years, the stage technology of the new house is already thirty years out of date, and seat-back subtitles, so pleasing at the Met, "had never been considered at Covent Garden, nor mentioned to the architect." (It was just announced that the indefatigably charitable Alberto Vilar will pick up the tab for the installation of seat-back titles at the new Covent Garden.)

Mr. Lebrecht was granted only "partial access" to the ROH archives. Indeed, when he wished to examine the archive file on Arnold Goodman, Harold Wilson's right-hand man and "the most influential fixer England had ever seen," Mr. Lebrecht drily notes that "With his usual skill, Goodman left no fingerprints. His file in the ROH archives is completely empty, cleared as if by order." Secrets must be guarded fanatically, even if they are anodyne and harmless:

> Before I could enter the archives, the board demanded that I obtain the approval of all past chairmen, one of whom refused access to the files pertaining to his period. I would later discover that he had little to hide. His response was typically that of an ROH grandee who saw no reason for the public to know what had been going on while he was in charge of a public-funded institution.

The appointment of the first General Administrator of the house, David Webster, 1945–1970, was symptomatic of the way things were to be. Once the manager of the Bon Marché department store in Liverpool and active in local music circles, Webster was drawn to London and told by the powers that be "to organize a national home for opera and ballet." An authoritarian musical amateur, Webster demanded total musical control, and it is appropiate to list the musical directors he would not consider: Beecham, Barbirolli, Malcolm Sargent, Albert Coates, Klemperer, Szell, Reiner, Erich Kleiber, and others. The young Leonard Bernstein conducted once in 1946 and was never invited back. "Any of these masters," Mr. Lebrecht notes, "was capable of raising an opera house from the foundations up, yet none was considered for Covent Garden." Webster chose an unknown Austrian exile: one Karl Rankl, unknown to all. Beecham's reaction was typical: "The appointment of an alien, and especially one bearing a German name, to the post of musical director of the British National Opera is so incredible that I have from time to time to remind myself that it has actually happened and is not some fantastic dream." The curse of provincialism initially hung over the house. The bracing slogan to "Buy British," that is, to use British singers over their better French, German, or Austrian counterparts made the first years of the ROH unnecessarily grim.

Yet after the expected demise of Karl Rankl, there have been many extraordinary triumphs. A list should include Erich Kleiber's *Wozzeck*, many stunning performances by Callas and Sutherland, the eras dominated by George Solti (a complete *Ring*, Schoenberg's *Moses und Aron*), Rafael Kubelik, Colin Davis, and Bernard Haitink, as well as the rise to stardom of Kiri Te Kanawa and Luciano Pavarotti. As for the Royal Ballet, one only need mention Dame Margot Fonteyn and her collaborations with Rudolf Nureyev and the choreography of Frederick Ashton, John Cranko, and Kenneth MacMillan. But the deficits grew to gargantuan proportions, much to the irritation and censure of the likes of Margaret Thatcher and John Major. Thanks to a generous infusion of funds from the National Lottery, the renovation was brought to a happy end, but the massive endowment needed for its independence has yet to be raised.

The most stunning sentence in Mr. Lebrecht's entire history is pronounced by Lord Drogheda. George Whyte was a young Hungarian-Jewish department store owner who offered to take charge of desperately needed fundraising for the ROH in exchange for a seat on the board. This was deemed to be too pushy an offer, and Drogheda offered a symptomatic, summary chastisement: "Never forget, George, what is an Englishman's by privilege, the Jew has to acquire by merit."

A few words about the late John Ardoin. At his death in March 2001, he had just retired after thirty-two years as the music critic of *The Dallas Morning News*. He was a well-esteemed presence in New York City music circles, as intermission guest on the Saturday afternoon Metropolitan Opera broadcasts, and as New York critic for *The Times* (of London) and *Opera* magazine. He was the author of some six books, two on Callas—*The Callas Legacy* and *Callas at Juilliard*, the latter work inspiring the playwright Terrence McNally to write his *Master Class*—and the definitive examination of the recorded legacy of Wilhelm Furtwängler. Ardoin was an extraordinarily honest critic—he wrote an unfavorable review of a performance by his friend Maria Callas in Dallas in 1974, and she never spoke to him again. He had just finished *Valery Gergiev and the Kirov* when he died suddenly from lymphoma. Had he lived, his next project was to have been an exhaustive examination of the recorded legacy of Leonard Bernstein.

Ardoin was nothing if not intrepid. Taking leave from the Dallas paper in 1995–1996, he moved to St.

Petersburg for the long winter in order to bear witness to the fortunes of the Mariinsky/Kirov theater. He enjoyed the complete cooperation of Valery Gergiev, the principal conductor and artistic director, and brought with him a friend who spoke fluent Russian. The archives of the house were open to Ardoin, should he be able to locate them. "The Mariinsky's historical papers and the designs of past productions have been scattered about town in at least a half a dozen buildings, and some had even wound up in Moscow." Indefatigable, Ardoin has given us four books in one—a portrait of the mercurial Gergiev, now a whirlwind presence in New York through his myriad activities at the Metropolitan Opera and performances with his own Kirov orchestra; a history of the theater since 1860; the personal journey of a Westerner learning a balletic and operatic repertory not often seen or heard in the West; and, finally, the story of an opera and ballet company desperately struggling in post-Communist Russia, bereft of the state support that had been dependable through the czars and Communists.

Ardoin sat through every performance possible—twenty-six different operas and twenty-eight ballets (all repeated, of course), four tours of Europe, and trips to Israel, Japan, and Denmark. Often, the stars were sent on tour and the vocal "Plan B" stayed home to perform, at times desultorily. There are three discrete orchestras—a ballet orchestra, an opera orchestra, and a tour orchestra, with personnel rotating among the three. For Ardoin, as for the reader, it is all dizzying in the extreme.

Ardoin's gifts as a musical critic—able to describe in words the peculiar power, majesty, or delicacy of each singer—make this a real treat for the inquiring musician and critic. Ardoin's ear for orchestral sonority and the ensemble in general is evident in his portrayals of the sound of an individual orchestra, and he roundly condemns some performances. For instance, after hearing nightly the vibrancy, oomph, and general dedication of the Kirov orchestra on their home grounds in St. Petersburg, Ardoin takes a flying trip to New York, accompanying Gergiev to the Met, where he will conduct Tchaikovsky's *Queen of Spades*. The much-vaunted Metropolitan Orchestra does not fare well:

> While the playing of the Met's orchestra was beautiful, precise, and professional, it lacked that hot-to-the-touch character of the Kirov's brass, tympani, and strings. Nor did the Met's musicians play with the sense of propulsion, the 100 percent plus the Kirov orchestra gives Gergiev night after night. The production was a grave disappointment.

An additional bonus to this extraordinary book is Ardoin's capacities, previously unknown to me, as a critic, appreciator, and describer of ballet performance. One has only to read his descriptions of particular performances of new (to Russia) works of Balanchine, and such old dependables as *La Bayadère*, *Le Corsaire*, *Romeo and Juliet*, or *The Sleeping Beauty*, to know how far-ranging were Ardoin's interests and talents, and what a loss his unexpected death is to the art of criticism.

In September 1997, Valery Gergiev was appointed principal guest conductor of the Metropolitan Opera. The final pages of both volumes by Johanna Fiedler and John Ardoin dedicate a good amount of ink as to the motives, hidden or obvious, behind such an appointment, and spend even more time contrasting the temperaments and conductorial and rehearsal techniques of Messrs. Gergiev and Levine—the latter tending toward the energetically Apollonian, the former much wilder, unpredictable, and very Dionysian. Ardoin, clearly the more discerning student of orchestral performance, tended to prefer Gergiev in spite of his helter-skelter habits, while Ms. Fiedler is, naturally, a Levine friend and advocate. There is, however, a moment in her book in which she crosses the line into something close to scurrilous hearsay. She quotes a "Met insider" who alleges that "With his icy shrewdness in assessing other conductors, Jimmy knows that the orchestra has little use for Gergiev. Jimmy knows Gergiev is a fraud, and either everyone else will catch on or they won't." Who is this "Met insider"? I am sorry that John Ardoin is not around to confront the wretch.

Such is the nature of writing about the opera world: gossip, ego, power struggles, etc. It disappears into the gloom when the curtain rises and the music begins.

March 2002

Authentically Bland

A FEW YEARS AGO a friend played for me a tape copy of an Edison cylinder recorded by Johannes Brahms in Vienna in 1889. Edison's agent in the city, Theo Wangemann, announces the date and place of the recording and that he is with "Doktor" Brahms himself. After a short pause, the playing begins. I could not at all identify the piece, since the scratch and swish seemed to drown out everything. My friend then conducted what was playing, and it jumped out at me—a snippet from the composer's "Hungarian Dance No. 1" in G minor. What was also evident was a rambunctious, free-wheeling pianism— what the young Artur Schnabel noted as Brahms's "creative vitality and wonderful carelessness." More scientifically, Jonathan Berger, of the Center for Computer Assisted Research in Music and Acoustics at Stanford University, after subjecting the Brahms cylinder to every conceivable scrutiny, notes a "liberal rubato, some protracted fermati, and improvisation at a number of points" and a tempo "considerably slower than any recent recording." My sense is that

Brahms was the kind of player who could play a piece all over again using only the notes he missed the first time around.

Timothy Day is curator of Western Art Music at the Sound Archive of the British Library in London. He has given us, at the very least, a study of the history and implications of recorded music from the late nineteenth century to our day, beginning with an inaccurate description of that Brahms cylinder right on the first page of his study. Much of this chronological treatment of the history of recordings—from cylinders to 78 rpm discs (first acoustically, then electrically recorded) to the 33 rpm LP vinyl record (mono, later stereo) and on to the compact disc revolution (not to mention DVD)—has been well covered in such works as Roland Gelatt's *Fabulous Phonograph* (1955, rev. 1977) and Guy A. Marco's *Encyclopedia of Recorded Sound in America* (1993). Moreover, the point of view given in Day's historical overview is decidedly English, not to say provincial. He leaves out many historical developments in the Forties and the Fifties on this side of the Atlantic that deserve scrutiny. For instance: how did the long-playing record develop within the CBS labs? Any reader of the various editions of David Hall's indispensable *Records in Review* (not consulted by Day) would know that, after Columbia's announcement of the LP revolution in the summer of 1948, RCA Victor, in a burst of foolish

---

* *A Century of Recorded Music*, by Timothy Day (Yale University Press).

commercial effrontery, decided that they would put out their own kind of discs, playing at 45 rpm and measuring only seven inches, which meant that only five minutes or so of music could be contained on each side. The long-playing record, measuring ten inches and later twelve inches, and able to contain twenty-five minutes of music, triumphed. Soon realizing that they had been vanquished in this matter, RCA Victor had to eat crow in January 1950 and ask for a license from Columbia Records, the patentee, to put out LP's, which it then proceeded to do along with everyone else, and the 45 rpm record was relegated to the jukebox where it belonged. But for a while, it was a toss-up between two goliaths, William Paley of CBS and "General" David Sarnoff of RCA. There is a real story here, but Day is not interested.

Similarly, while he is careful to point out the technological advances in recording on tape brought about by Decca/London, EMI, Deutsche Grammophon, and Telefunken, both in England and on the continent, he never mentions the revolutionary recording technique of C. Robert Fine and David Hall of Mercury Records in the United States—the simple device of hanging one Telefunken microphone over the podium, resulting in a series of still stunning and still revered recordings. The idea was that it was a conductor's business to balance an orchestra, not an engineer with knob in hand after the fact.

Day is right to emphasize the role of the record producer, and he expectedly (and properly) outlines the achievements of three men—Fred Gaisberg, Walter

Legge, and John Culshaw. Each is renowned—Gaisberg for his intrepid recording of Caruso in a Milan hotel room in 1902 and for recording Chaliapin, John McCormack, Mischa Elman, Kreisler, Schnabel and Casals, not to mention two great recordings made just before World War II, the Dvořák Cello Concerto with Casals, Szell, and the Czech Philharmonic, and a still inimitable Mahler Ninth with Bruno Walter and the Vienna Philharmonic. If Gaisberg was saintly and self-effacing, his disciple Walter Legge was nasty and autocratic, as befits the husband of Elisabeth Schwarzkopf. Easily the most hated man in the business, Legge was characterized in memorable fashion by Sir Thomas Beecham as "a mass of egregious fatuity." Perhaps, but Legge was the sole creator of the Philharmonia Orchestra, the genius behind Angel Records, the discoverer of Herbert von Karajan. Against all odds, Legge certainly got things done—*Tristan und Isolde* with Flagstad and Furtwängler, the Karajan/Schwarzkopf *Rosenkavalier*, the innumerable late recordings of Otto Klemperer, the great series of Viennese operettas, the championing of Lipatti—the list goes on and on. More convivially, the scholarly and reserved John Culshaw is renowned for one of the great sonic achievements of the stereo era—Wagner's monumental *Ring der Nibelungen*, with the best singers of the day and the impassioned collaboration of the Vienna Philharmonic Orchestra under Georg Solti.

Day is quite justified in giving these three their due, but, as an evocative writer and a critic with insight into people, he has stiff competition from Norman

Lebrecht. In *Who Killed Classical Music?* (1997), Lebrecht, the music columnist for *The Daily Telegraph*, wrote about this same trio of producers with a panache and flair that Day cannot manage. As for the same kind of visionaries in the United States, Day does mention once in passing the seminal figure of Goddard Lieberson (head of Columbia Records), but Lebrecht has more detail:

> [Lieberson] signed Stravinsky to record his entire musical output, retrieved Charles Ives from oblivion, lured the iconoclastic pianists Vladimir Horowitz and Glenn Gould [whose signing was actually the work of Lieberson's lieutenant David Oppenheim] to the label, protected the slow-selling Duke Ellington. His original-cast album of *My Fair Lady* sold five million copies in 1957 and helped pay for comprehensive Schoenberg and Webern editions.

The recordings of the Bernstein era with the New York Philharmonic and of such great Broadway shows as *Porgy and Bess* and *South Pacific* were also Lieberson's doing. Little of this information is in Day's book.

Day goes to great lengths to discuss topics that are of a very peculiar and particular interest to an English music lover—the changing timbres over the years of the King's College Choir or whether most of English Renaissance choir music is being sung a minor third too low. In a subsection entitled "Composers listen to recordings," there is a whole series of speculations

concerning particular English composers' first en-
counters with gramophone records, and their possible
influence. In the case of John Tavener, for instance,

> when he was three . . . he played over and over again
> a record made in 1929 of 250 Manchester school-
> children singing Purcell's "Nymphs and Shepherds,"
> and his biographer suggests that this is early evidence
> of his enduring love for high and pure voices and for
> ritual and repetition, perhaps a defining moment.

Maybe so, maybe not.

The book is also full of odd juxtapositions of intriguing subjects. In chapter III, "Changes in Performing Styles Recorded," a section on "Performance
Style in Fourteenth-Century Chansons" is followed by
"Changing Styles in Webern Performance." All prices
for 78 discs are given in pre-World War I shillings,
pounds, and guineas, with no table of monetary
equivalency in today's dollars. In general, the study
seems unnecessarily discontinuous in the organization
of its historical materials.

There is, however, and this is to be taken as a very
weighty "however," another book hidden within this
historical overview. Day has given his study a subtitle,
which I purposely omitted from the heading of this
review: "Listening to Musical History." The question
is what has been the effect of the gradual accumula-
tion of past recorded musical performance on the
contemporary performer. And in that sense, we are
back to the Brahms cylinder. It is not just that Brahms

played his composition with reckless gusto and panache; Day avers that before the recording era *all* conductors, soloists, and singers considered performance as something close to an opportunity for improvisation and on-the-spot reworking of musical texts. It was absolute re-creation, the only reference point being a possible prior audition of the same piece somewhere else. Day describes in rich detail how composers such as Elgar and Rachmaninoff recorded versions of their compositions that were at considerable variance with the musical text in question. Moreover, as Day so convincingly shows, there is no evidence that the distance between the musical score and the sonic realization back then was at all perturbing to the composers in question. After all, they were right there in the studio, in charge of everything.

One of the largest implications of recordings is that they constitute an ongoing record of sonic self-consciousness. This aspect of the power of the new technology is amusingly pointed out by Day when he describes the Gaisberg sessions with the sixty-two-year-old Adelina Patti in December 1905. After performing various arias, she threw kisses at the recording machine and was heard to exclaim: "Oh! My God!! Now I understand why I am Patti!! Yes!! What a voice!! What an artist!! I understand everything now!!" On a more serious level, the older artists before the microphone displayed, according to Day, an "improvisatory nature, the slight air of disorderliness, of spontaneity, which disconcerts a modern listener most of all."

The famous recordings of Beethoven quartets by the Busch Quartet are performances of four distinct musical personalities interacting, as they might express it, rather than the smooth, effortless, meticulous and precisely coordinated and integrated ensemble speaking with one voice characteristic of the 1990's.

(Here, Day is obviously referring to the antiseptic, wholly concerted performing style typical of such groups as the Alban Berg Quartet, the Emerson Quartet, and the Vermeer Quartet.) Day rightly points out that "a listener's expectations in the concert hall, in live performances, are based on the standards achieved or seemingly achieved in performances on discs." Today many old orchestral practices sound wrong, or just sloppy. For instance, conductors such as Felix Weingartner and Wilhelm Furtwängler favored arppegiating opening chords, such as the first bars of the Beethoven Third or Seventh—the lower choirs would enter a millisecond before the rest of the orchestra, resulting in a rush of sound rather than a simultaneous chordal blast. These are out of the question today. As an uninitiated friend remarked, "They can't even *start* together!!"

Day concludes that "Recordings have clearly documented the taming, as some might see it, the moderating, the cooling, the classicizing of performing styles." The propagation of gramophone recordings has also accompanied a grand tendency toward objectivization in the arts in the twentieth century. Exactitude, without "personal" stylistic interjection, is valued now more than ever, everything must be "authentic." Day suggests that the gramophone in its totality has forced something of a cowed historical consciousness upon all younger performers' and conductors' minds as they ply their craft, and this has resulted in a greater and greater musical literalness, or worse, a blandness both in musical performance and in recording. It would seem that during this now century-long process in which gramophone recordings have played such a key role, much has been gained, and even more has been irrevocably lost.

April 2001

Orpheus in Hell

TODAY, the exhortative power of music for political ends is a forgotten topic. But as anyone who was alive during World War II in the United States remembers, things were different then. This brand of musical motivation was all around us. Now, hurtling as we are into the new millennium, we are as far from the stirring "God Bless America" as sung by Kate Smith as we are from Marc Blitzstein's *Airborne Symphony*, Randall Thompson's *Testament of Freedom*, Earl Robinson's *Ballad for Americans*—even Aaron Copland's *Lincoln Portrait*, though the latter work still appears on musical programs around the Fourth of July. During the war, there was a commonality that permeated all echelons of society, and the music that emanated from that collective sense of purpose came in all sorts of guises, from the above-mentioned musical artifacts to War Bond rallies to broadcasts by Toscanini, Glenn Miller, and Woody Guthrie.

There was no cultural commissar in Washington or grand propaganda machine that orchestrated this effort, though there were a few American aspirants to the role of boosterish exhorter, at least in the realm of literature. Edmund Wilson, in his essay "Archibald MacLeish and the Word" (collected in *Classics and Commercials*), noted in 1940 that MacLeish, then in his role as Librarian of Congress, descended to the level of asking writers that they lay off pessimism and nay-saying for the duration. Optimism was the order of the day. In an address given to the American Association for Adult Education more than a year before Pearl Harbor, MacLeish insinuated that "perhaps the luxury of complete confession, the uttermost despair, the farthest doubt, should be denied themselves by writers living in any but the most orderly and settled times." (Question to MacLeish: exactly *when* are times orderly and settled?) Wilson's response to this fantastic request by the Librarian of Congress was both stupefied and succinct: "It is hard to see how any person to whom literature was even for a moment real could have written the sentence I have quoted." If we extend, in an imaginative flight, the purview of MacLeish's diktat to classical music, one trembles at the thought of an infinite series of bright, heroic allegros and sundry other celebrations of future sunny morns that might have been scribbled out by American composers who found themselves earnestly fulfilling MacLeish's injunction.

Art and politics don't mix. But the point is that MacLeish was just dispensing bromides. He was not suggesting sinister political moves against those he thought of as miscreants in art: the irresponsible and nihilistic novelists who were not "with the program."

Things were decidedly different in the Germany of the 1930s and 1940s. Hitler handed over to Joseph Goebbels the activities of censor and cultural commissar in 1933, creating the Reich Culture Chamber (RKK), which rigorously supervised all aspects of cultural life—radio, theater, film, creative writing, the press, and music. Although the outlines of the manipulation of musical life in Hitler's Germany, as brought about by the subsection of the RKK called the Reich Music Chamber (RMK), are well known, until this decade no scholar has had the energy and equanimity to deal with such a monstrous topic in all its ramifications, and to try to ask and answer a few simple questions. What did the Nazis want from music? What were their aims, aside from the most obvious elimination of Jewish "music and musicians"? How is it that so many musicians fell under their spell?

The aims of the Nazis were evident from the start. German culture had gone astray, and they were going to put things right by means of a purgative, purifying process. In music, this meant idealizing consonant tonality and driving out all elements not traditionally "German" in their view—the anathemata were serial, "dodecaphonic" music; Jewish music and musicians; gypsy music; and jazz in all its forms.

It is a good moment for an appraisal of this subject, so fraught with snares on all sides, because Oxford University Press has just published Michael Kater's *Composers of the Nazi Era: Eight Portraits* (Oxford University Press) which discusses the political difficulties and evasions of Werner Egk, Paul Hindemith,

Kurt Weill, Karl Amadeus Hartmann, Carl Orff, Hans Pfitzner, Arnold Schoenberg, and Richard Strauss. This is the final volume of a trilogy, which Kater, who teaches at the Center for German and European Studies at York University, Toronto, began in 1992 with *Different Drummers: Jazz in the Culture of Nazi Germany*. His second volume, *The Twisted Muse: Musicians and Their Music in the Third Reich* (1997), concentrated on conductors and instrumentalists. These books are to be commended for their energetic scholarship and the measured tone of critical prudence and judiciousness. It could not have been easy.

As Kater suggests, music has always played a preponderant role in German culture. "Certainly until 1945," he writes, "the Germans as a people, not only in the Hitlerian *Völkisch* sense, defined themselves and their history decisively through *Kultur*—they said they always had it, and nobody else did." German music was Kultur, and vice versa. Concomitantly, the only good music was German music. "[I]n their collective view, this is what set them apart from materialistic British money-bags, degenerate French hedonists, insensitive American pragmatists, work-shirking Italian fools, and the alcoholized denizens of a half-Asiatic Russian Empire."

Music was marshalled for the political cause with far more depth and intensity than that imposed upon the other arts. The German composer most prized by the Nazis was Richard Wagner, with his heady admixture of art and politics. Musical nationalism is evident to any listener to *Die Meistersinger von Nürnberg*, while German racial superiority is vaunted throughout his critical writings, above all in his "What is German?," *My Life*, and *Judaism and Music*. There is no question, Kater observes,

> that Hitler, continuing his rise to power in the mid-to-late 1920's, considered himself Wagner's direct successor, a man of genius and a hero who would save the German people, who in turn were defined and united by a purity of blood. . . . To Hitler, Richard Wagner was prophet, archetypal German polymath, and artist as well as political leader.

Finally, "National Socialism was anchored in the works of Wagner." Hitler dixit.

As for the fate of any ordinary German musician, Jewish or not, trying to make a living in this maelstrom, the statistics are daunting. By 1933, there were over ninety thousand active musicians working or trying to find work in Germany. Fewer than half of these artists were devoted to the so-called classics, or serious music. As for musical venues, Berlin had three opera houses, forty theaters, twenty cabarets, and several concert halls. There were locales for variety revues, the most famous being the Scala, capable of seating three thousand customers for each show. Hamburg and Munich were close runners-up in musical activity. But because of the 1929 crash, musicians had been cast out into the streets in droves.

By 1933 even some members of the well-endowed Berlin Philharmonic had suffered salary cuts of 40 percent. Jewish musicians of the highest caliber were gradually decertified in increasing numbers during the thirties as unacceptable by the RMK. To make the dreadful story as short as possible, a German musicologist in the early 1980s estimated that, of the above-numbered working musicians in 1933 Germany, a mere 465 musicians were able to emigrate to the United States during the Hitler period—most of them Jews.

Within the Nazi imagination the enemies of German *Seele* ("soul") in music were various and legion, and they had to be dealt with energetically. One might start, as did Professor Kater in his first volume, with the most un-German of all manifestations of modernism—jazz. Simply put, to the Nazis, jazz was detrimental to the future of German music, and it had to be rooted out of German musical life. The younger generation of German "classical" composers influenced by jazz—Paul Hindemith, Kurt Weill, Ernst Krenek—were thus automatically beyond the pale. But jazz had been a godsend to German modernists of all genres. It was going to rejuvenate classical music, which had lately gone stale. It was the "music of this decade" and the "incarnation of American vitalism." It was non-hierarchical, a musical emancipation from stodginess—a "school of democracy for Germans." The Bauhaus had its own student jazz band. George Grosz and Paul Klee adored jazz. Hindemith's teacher, Dr. Bernhard Sekles, instituted a jazz course at the

Frankfurt Conservatory in early 1928, teaching rhythm, improvisation, and ensemble playing.

But for the followers of the National Socialist movement, jazz was a doubly nefarious genre, since its practitioners constituted, in the words of Alfred Rosenberg, the Nazi's chief ideologue, a "Jewish-Negro plot against German culture." In a startling scholarly find, Kater carefully describes the poster for the infamous "Degenerate Music" exhibit in Dussel-dorf in 1937, "featuring a monkeylike Negro, decorated with the Star of David, tooting on a saxophone." (It is worth noting that, according to Kater, the Marxist philosopher Theodor W. Adorno, later a scourge of all things authoritarian, in the 1930s "enthused over the prospect of the Nazi authorities forbidding [jazz] altogether.") Jazz got all the blame—serialism, atonality, and (Hindemith's) New Objectivity were the fault of the all-pervasive jazz culture. Josephine Baker, Al Jolson in *The Jazz Singer*, *The Blue Angel* with music by the immensely popular Weintraub Syncopators (soon wisely to exile themselves from Germany with their pianist Franz Waxman, later of Hollywood fame), all brought on fits of Goebbels' wrath. The Nazis had the idea that a jazz player or fan was unreliable. As one storm trooper exclaimed after the failed attempt on Hitler's life, "Anything that starts with Ellington ends with an assassination attempt on the Führer!"

As early as 1932, the Von Papen regime had banned the employment of any "colored" musician, and the decree was enforced. When, in January 1935, the

American black tenor saxophonist Coleman Hawkins was scheduled to tour Germany with the English "sweet" dance band led by Jack Hylton, the regime forbade his presence in German dance halls. Hawkins was marooned in Holland for the duration of the band's tour in Germany, and so we have Von Papen and Goebbels to thank for the splendid recordings he made with the innocuous Dutch band called "The Ramblers Dance Orchestra." As for the numerous Jewish musicians within and without Germany in the realm of "light music," the restrictions were ever more stringent, but with a few amusing slips. Benny Goodman, "jazz musician, director of a jazz band in London," was of course listed in a February 1937 list of forbidden Jewish musicians, but his erstwhile competitor on the jazz clarinet, Artie Shaw (born Arthur Arshawsky), was not because "the Nazis believed him to be the son of 'former Irish music critic' George Bernard Shaw!" Connections always helped, some muddled through, but there was the constant threat of dismissal or worse—a knock on the door. It is only fair to note that Richard Strauss, otherwise serene in his Garmisch redoubt, was eased out of the RMK presidency in 1935 because he would not decertify or dismiss any Jewish musician.

The Twisted Muse, Kater's second volume, trod on more familiar ground, but here too he presented an abundance of fresh material. Particularly depressing is the spectacle of a whole raft of mediocre composers given inordinate attention all because of their political reliability. Has anyone today ever heard a note of music by Paul Graener or Max Trapp? They were the white hope of German music, while all music related to the so-called "Second Viennese School" (Schoenberg, Berg, Webern) was utterly *verboten*, yet another aspect of the sinister plot to destroy Holy German Music. And there is the spectacle of the constant jockeying for Der Führer's attention on the part of such otherwise distinguished conductors as Wilhelm Furtwängler, Clemens Krauss, and Hans Knappertsbusch. Professor Kater also explores the figure of Herbert von Karajan with not especially pleasant results. Richard Osborne, the author of a recent biography of Karajan, has severely criticized the accuracy of Kater's portrait of the conductor. Still, one senses that Kater has given us cool, not at all vengeful, treatments of the likes of Elisabeth Schwarzkopf, Karl Böhm, Hans Rosbaud, and the pianists Wilhelm Backhaus, Edwin Fischer, Wilhelm Kempff, and Walter Gieseking. There are innumerable other, major and minor, figures.

There are terrible things to be seen in these pages—the spectacle of Anton Webern reading *Mein Kampf* as late as 1940, finding it "exhilarating," and following "every German victory on the Western front with great enthusiasm." After all, Webern was a composer denigrated mercilessly by the Nazis as "degenerate." Equally absurd and depressing is the spectacle of Lorenzo da Ponte's role as librettist for Mozart's operas being expunged from the musical scores published in the Reich, or the rewriting of Handel's superb oratorio *Judas Maccabeus* to rid it of "Biblical,

Jewish" trappings and sending it back into the Nazi concert halls under the title *Commander*! And what to make of Carl Orff knowingly composing a score to supplant the incomparable incidental music composed by Felix Mendelssohn for *A Midsummer Night's Dream*? Orff's pounding, heavily rhythmic music, as exemplified in his big "hit" of 1937, *Carmina Burana*, was precisely the kind of music the Nazis wanted.

Of particular interest in *The Twisted Muse* is the fourth chapter, "Music in the Institutions." This has to do with the decline of *Hausmusik*, the emphasis on archaic impulses and new uses for the recorder, the guitar, and joy-in-nature choral singing fostered by the Hitler Youth (obligatory for all youths between ten and eighteen by 1939). The aim was twofold: to utilize music, with its ideological and character-building potential, in order to raise better leaders—a kind of perverted *paideia*—and to infiltrate the existing musical establishment and turn them into political singing groups. "With one fell swoop, [such renowned choirs as] the Thomaner-Chor of Leipzig, the Dresdner Kreuzchor, the Wiener Sängerknaben, and the Regensburger Domspatzen were collectively taken over by Hitler Youth, without so much as being asked." By 1944, there were some nine-hundred Hitler Youth musical aggregations.

On a final note of musical sacrilege, the organist at Bach's church in Leipzig, Günther Ramin, who is now remembered as the mentor of Karl Richter, the famed director of the Munich Bach Choir, took part in many Nazi celebrations, not the least of which was as organist at the Nuremberg rally of 1936. He played on a modest instrument of 16,000 pipes, 220 registers, and five manuals, all amplified by giant loud-speakers—Albert Speer's empty architectural bombast in the form of a "musical" instrument.

Composers of the Nazi Era is, in many ways, a summa of the problems that have obsessed Kater for the past decade. Although he touches on many issues already discussed, he also offers many new insights and scholarly discoveries. For instance, it is a matter of record that Richard Strauss signed a defamation against Thomas Mann, on the basis of Mann's pondered consideration of the work of Wagner, which became the lecture "Sufferings and Greatness of Richard Wagner," delivered in Munich in 1933 and subsequently in Amsterdam, Brussels, and Paris. In many ways, this work was Mann's adieu to Germany—he emigrated, first to Switzerland, then to the United States, shortly afterwards. The screed against Mann was probably authored by the arch-nationalist conductor Hans Knappertsbusch, an old hand at Munich intrigues, and Strauss has always been severely criticized for joining in the anti-Mann fray. But here we have Professor Kater, who, in his researches in the Strauss archive in Garmisch, has come up with documentation, "which I have found only recently," suggesting that Strauss had not read Mann's text, and that he foolishly signed the protest less for ideological than for personal reasons; he had always harbored a visceral dislike of Mann, considering him "a boring patrician." There is evidence of a possible retraction, but it was too late. The long story told by Kater shows the results of such diligence. Needless to say, the matter is still hardly flattering to Strauss.

Kater also gives us a portrait of Paul Hindemith, "The Reluctant Emigré," which contrasts notably with that given us by the composer's colleague at Yale during the war years, Luther Noss, who in *Paul Hindemith in the United States* (1989) painted a placid picture of the exiled German composer, energetic teacher, and reformer, content and productive in New Haven until his sudden resignation from Yale in 1948. Kater has a completely different take on Hindemith, his relationship to German *Kultur*, and the decision to leave Yale so suddenly. Kater senses a musical mind indelibly bound to Germany and its culture, a participant in the RMK under Richard Strauss, who in turn admired the younger upstart for his wide-ranging knowledge, all-round musicianship, and incredible proficiency on the major instruments of the orchestra, but who didn't care for the younger man's music. It turns out that Hindemith was reluctant in the extreme to emigrate, and did so only after no other possibilities were open to him, well after Furtwängler had defended him and even Strauss had offered to take the libretto of Hindemith's opera *Mathis der Maler* to Goebbels, to show the opera's suitability for the aims of the new regime. Kater does not even think of Hindemith as an émigré, though geographically he most certainly was one.

Kater's conclusions are implicit: "One and all—

musicians and singers, composers and conductors, all of whom had to make a living as artists in the Third Reich—emerged in May 1945 severely tainted, with their professional ethos violated and their music often compromised: gray people against a landscape of gray." Although Kater implies no ur-cause to so much immorality in the realm of music, it seems to lie evident throughout all three volumes—the chauvinistic, increasingly narrow definitions of "what is German" converted into a paranoiac, exclusionary musical myopia, which in turn was enforced by sanctioned governmental violence. All this stems from insane hauteur and hubris on the matter of music and Germany. As Wagner once said: "the German has the exclusive right to be called 'musician.'" Oh?

In his last chapter, "Composers in the Postwar Era," Kater treats us to a searing critique of the "denazification" proceedings as they were to apply to particular composers from among the eight under consideration, where outright fabrications, lies, and guile ruled the defense case in each particular proceeding. The self-portraiture by Carl Orff and Werner Egk as resistance fighters against the Nazis is particularly galling. Not surprisingly, given the rush to "get things over with" impelled by the new threat from the Soviet Union, the ineptness of the prosecutions only compounded the whitewash, and so it is understandable, even inevitable, that all concerned got off light and easy, no problem.

Today Archibald MacLeish's exhortation to writers of the Thirties seems quaintly innocent, no matter how foolish. But the diktats emanating from the German Propaganda Ministry regarding music are obviously retrogressive commands to go back in time to the primitive bark and shout. At its worst, they wanted a version in sound of what Jorge Luis Borges called "the game of energetic barbarism." Michael Kater has given us a careful prose description of this sinister musical atavism.

October 2000

At Last, the Promised Land?

O N SATURDAY, February 20, 1999, most of the usual weekly listeners to the Texaco-sponsored broadcasts from the Metropolitan Opera cannot have been pleased by the sounds emanating from their radios. For the first time, Arnold Schoenberg's opera *Moses und Aron* was broadcast to an audience noted for their decades of loyal and fervent support of operas like *La Traviata* or *La Bohème*. True, a surprising number of seats at the Met had been sold for a prior performance on February 11 and the ovations on that occasion had been hearty and vociferous, but one can wager that many listening to the Saturday matinee broadcast quickly voted with their fingers and moved to another location on the dial.

Sixty-seven years after its composition, *Moses und Aron* is still a barrage of sound, a sonic avalanche. The spelling of both names in the title is unusual. As the annotator Michael Steinberg has pointed out, "Moses" is "Mose" in German, "Aaron" is "Aaron," as in English. The two *a*'s in Aaron's name have been shortened to one *a*, while an additional *s*, borrowed from the English spelling of "Moses," has been added, making both spellings foreign to the German reader, unsettling and perhaps alien to those used to Martin Luther's version. In any case, the resulting twelve letters match, at least numerically, the twelve-tone row that governs the permutations of the whole opera. The fact that Schoenberg was born on September 13, 1874 and was fervently triskaidekaphobic must have produced a sense of foreboding from childhood on. As a composer, he was always seen (and above all by himself) as the heroic outsider. Many thought of him as a pariah and musical defiler of the three B's of German musical tradition, while others, admittedly a minority of music lovers, considered him a musical Moses, a giver of laws. It is difficult to evoke the fury and derision occasioned by his music in the early Vienna days, though the treatment accorded to his mentor and friend Gustav Mahler must have steeled him for the worst. For instance, at the first performance of Schoenberg's magnificent String Quartet No. 2, the review of the work was printed in the "Crime" section of the *New Vienna Daily* of December 22, 1908, the critic suggesting that the music sounded like "a convocation of cats."

Schoenberg himself never heard any part of *Moses und Aron* performed. Promises were made but never kept. The first performances were in Switzerland in 1957, six years after he died. The instrumental, choral and vocal demands are even now at the very limit of contemporary technical execution; only major opera houses can possibly do it justice. Sir Georg Solti, a master technician who delighted in the complexity of "new" music, noted, "I remember so vividly the fears and anxiety I had when I first studied the score of *Moses und Aron* in 1965. I found it unbelievably complicated, and thought I would never manage to learn it. But since then I have performed the work over twenty times." The difficulties that accompany the initial hearing and perception of the work derive not only from Schoenberg's by now well-known pan-tonal musical vocabulary, but also in the wild mélange of forces needed to realize the grand vision that the opera contains. *Moses und Aron* requires a large and highly energized orchestra, a choir that has mastered both traditional singing parts and *sprechstimme*, a kind of musical declamation. There are highly demanding parts for both Moses, who is listed as a "speaker" in the score, and Aron, a *bel canto* tenor. Other supporting singers of considerable technical agility are needed, along with a corps de ballet essential to realize the sonic and visual showpiece of the second act, the orgy/dance around the Golden Calf.

There is also the matter of Schoenberg's own libretto, drawn freely from well-known passages in the Books of Exodus and Numbers, but with notable alterations and reformulations of the biblical story. Unlike so many librettos, it is not a "weak sister" in the relation between words and music, where the words are there just enough for the characters to launch into song. As Auden put it, "libretto . . . offers as many opportunities as possible for the characters to be swept off their feet by placing them in situations which are too tragic or fantastic for 'words.'" This is an ongoing balancing act, first announced by that eighteenth century saying "prima la musica poi le parole"—though some composers preferred the reversal of these same terms.

In Schoenberg's case, both words and music are at once inextricably bound to and wildly divergent from each other. This is the quandary which is the axis of the libretto: the irreconcilability between idea and representation of that same idea, between archetype and its expression, between the "one, infinite, omnipresent one, unperceived and inconceivable God" and his verbal and pictorial earthly representation. Schoenberg has done something rare for an opera composer; he has fashioned a libretto of both religious and philosophical resonance, an opera for a thinking audience, and he makes it work on stage by means of a clever dramaturgy and carefully thought-out staging. He had to manhandle the Bible a bit. For instance, the substance of the first act is the miracles: Moses's staff turned into a snake, Moses's hand becoming leprous and being cured, the waters of the Jordan turned to blood. In the Bible, these are miracles wrought by God. In the libretto, it is the showman Aron who does the job.

But at the most elemental level of Schoenberg's intent, before any echoes or ramifications of the literary libretto are teased out, the basic quandary demands that Moses should not and must not sing under any circumstances (except for an inexplicable nine bars in

Act I). He is closer to immeasurable silence than to idle words or song. He must express himself gruffly in *sprechstimme*, telling all of the mission given him by God. He does not yet know he will fail. But, Aron, his "mouth" and worldly agent, should and must sing with all the florid *bel canto* roulades he can muster. He sings almost tonal arias. His is the power of word and song over the masses. As a betrayer of the extraordinary to the commonplace, he is just the man for a rally or a grand convocation. He is, alas, a leader (ein Führer), a Jim Jones of another time. The opera was finished on March 10, 1932. In Germany, yet another kind of Führer was soon to become chancellor.

Biblical preoccupations were not at the forefront of Schoenberg's formative years. He was born into an emancipated Jewish family in Vienna: his mother came from a Prague cantorial family while his father was a simple shoemaker from Slovakia. Schoenberg was something of a radical free-thinker and an enthusiast of the excoriations of Karl Kraus, the apocalyptic journalist who had already described the Vienna of his time as the "experiment station for the end of the world." Schoenberg was "never anti-religious but never really unreligious either," and in 1912, he noted in a letter that "I have been wanting to write an oratorio on the following subject: modern man . . . despite having been an atheist, still having in him some residue of ancient belief (in the form of superstition) wrestles with God and finally succeeds in finding God and becoming religious. Learning to pray!" The increasing anti-Semitism in both Austria and Germany, the attacks against him as a "Jewish" composer, all culminated in his "re-entry into the community of Israel" in Paris on July 24, 1933, with Marc Chagall as the only witness.

In a notable letter to Alban Berg, Schoenberg affirmed, "Everything I have written has a certain inner likeness to myself." Indeed, after the composition of *Moses und Aron* (1930–1932) and the beginning of his permanent exile in the United States, Schoenberg almost single-handedly tried to organize the salvation of European Jewry by means of a "Jewish Unity Party," which would negotiate with the German government for the orderly exile of emigrés to a homeland still to be found. Schoenberg said he would "sacrifice [his] art to the Jewish cause." In this fantastic propoganda campaign which he himself would lead, he needed to "lease an airplane permitting me to complete as quickly as possible the travels which it would enable me to undertake, a mobile home, a special broadcasting staff, disc recordings of my important speeches, sound films." He would speak with Roosevelt. He hoped for the enrollment of four million Jews contributing one mark a month for the cause. This political program, called "A Four-Point Program for Jewry," was drafted in the first months of his exile in Brookline, Massachusetts in 1933 and given final form in California in 1938. It came to naught. By the time of the Kristallnacht of November 1938, Schoenberg/Moses, "realizing the utter futility of his political effort, turned increasing inward."

Schoenberg's depiction of Moses might also be thought of as a self-portrait of himself as the reviled musical revolutionary. He sensed his mission as the bringer of a salvational musical system that would lead harmonic usage out of the dead end of tonality vitiated by excessive chromaticism. Schoenberg's twelve-tone expansion of musical language was one that was taken up by his "disciples," Anton Webern and Alban Berg, with varying degrees of rigor, at times with a language veering toward tonality (Berg), in other instances an even greater musical economy and manipulation of silence (Webern). Ironically, this expanded language was later employed by the more popular Igor Stravinsky, but only after the master himself had died. It is not impossible that the shadow of Stravinsky among other targets lurks behind the facile changeling that is Schoenberg's Aron. Schoenberg was not wont to forgive backsliders.

Ever suspicious of executants of his work who might have wayward or idiosyncratic ideas about the staging of this opera, Schoenberg filled the orchestral score with the most specific stage instructions imaginable, with the idea that "I wanted to leave as little as possible to those new despots of the theatrical art, the producers, and even to envisage the choreography as far as I'm able to." He does this, above all, in the orgy scene around the Golden Calf, but even Cecil B. DeMille would have blanched at the specifics: "During Aron's last speech processions of laden camels, asses, horses, porters and wagons enter the stage from different directions, bringing offerings as of gold, grain, skins of wine and oil . . . the animals are decorated and wreathed . . . butchers with large knives enter and with wild leaps dance around the animals." There is more. Four naked virgins, that is, "naked to the extent that the rules and necessities of the stage allow and require" are sacrificed—"the priests thrust the knives into their hearts. The blood is caught in receptacles. The priests pour it forth on the altar." Mr. Graham Vick, in charge of this Metropolitan Opera staging, gave us a Golden Calf scene that is an appropriately orgiastic crowd pleaser, sans animals and droppings, but with some blood. Faithful also to the "despotism" decried by Schoenberg, Mr. Vick and his set and costume designer Paul Brown gave us a band of well over one hundred oppressed choristers/Israelites dressed as Hasidim apparently out for a toot at a Brooklyn deli or venting their rage at City Hall. The orgiasts themselves had a Brechtian cast, cavorting in mangy furs out of Goodwill, flashbulbs popping, plastic surgeons doing their thing, all very glitzy. Pity the muscle-bound men of the Met chorus, who had to prance about bare-chested for the Dance of the Butchers, smearing themselves with offal and dreck, heartily bellowing all the time. These are the producer's importations, and why not, I suppose; anything goes these days. Haven't we seen Wotan singing in a tuxedo?

What is of final import is the visually impressive ochre sets of the blasted wastes, and, of course, the transmittal of both word and music under the leadership of the demonically possessed James Levine. Philip

Langridge's oily Aron was already well known through his 1985 recording with Sir Georg Solti; equally impressive and stentorian was the Moses of John Tomlinson who poured forth his *sprechstimme* with force and eloquence; with fulsome beard, he made Charlton Heston look mighty puny.

May 1999

The Virgilian Agenda

AN INFORMAL POLL among friends in New York (some musicians, some not) points up considerable divergence of opinion about the present stature of Virgil Thomson (1896–1989), the American composer and critic who is now the subject of an incisive and not at all hagiographical biography by Anthony Tommasini, a music critic for *The New York Times*.[*]

For a start, it should be said that Virgil Thomson's reputation is now based primarily on two things. First, he was the composer of two influential American operas written in collaboration with Gertrude Stein: *Four Saints in Three Acts* (1934) and *The Mother of Us All* (1947). The second source of his current reputation is the witty yet unremittingly highbrow music criticism he wrote for *The New York Herald Tribune* between 1940 and the fall of 1954. Thomson's position as a serious composer who also

---

* *Virgil Thomson: Composer on the Aisle*, by Anthony Tommasini (Norton).

held a critic's post on a major daily newspaper makes him a rare if not, indeed, unique case in the annals of American cultural life. Certainly, nothing like it could happen today.

Both of the above-mentioned operas, along with his last opera, *Lord Byron* (1972), are now available on the compact disc format, and a selection from his books, *Tribune* criticism, and later contributions to *The New York Review of Books* can still be found in *A Virgil Thomson Reader*, edited by Thomson himself with an introduction by John Rockwell (Houghton Mifflin, 1981).

As I say, there was little consensus among my correspondents about the present stature of the work of Virgil Thomson as a composer. The mere mention of his name to one distinguished and well-known contemporary American composer brought a dismissive guffaw, followed by a short but devastating tirade full of derision for Thomson as a composer. This same irritated composer did cut Thomson some slack as a music critic, however, voicing guarded approval for the musical judgments pronounced in the *Tribune* and elsewhere.

A few—very few—others had vague memories of performances of the once well-known orchestral suites drawn from Thomson's ventures into film music, the works that still occasionally show up (sometimes at Pops concerts) known as *The Plow That Broke the Plains*, *The River*, or *The Louisiana Story*. One friend thought of Thomson now only as a caustic critical presence, to be read for his panache and strut no matter what the subject. Going further afield, there were curious lacunae, studied slights, apparent forgetfulness. Consider: in a work so inclusive as the revised and expanded version of Robert Craft's *Stravinsky: The Chronicle of a Friendship* (Vanderbilt University Press, 1994)—a book in which everyone in the then reigning cultural worlds of both East and West coasts gets mentioned at least once—the name of Virgil Thomson does not appear in the index, although he is a very visible and a not especially flattering presence in a few episodes of Craft's *Chronicle*.

A bad slip on the part of the indexer? I think not. He appears as "Virgil Thomason" in Jan Swafford's *Charles Ives: A Life with Music* (Norton, 1996). Not a good sign. Mr. Tommasini, who knew Thomson well toward the end of his life and did a doctoral dissertation on Thomson's piano "portraits," must have heard much testimony from the master himself about how quickly some artists and composers are marginalized or decanonized. Mr. Tommasini's anecdote on this subject early in his book is both astonishing and utterly convincing. Here it is, *in toto*:

On a 1992 edition of the *Texaco Opera Quiz*, the popular intermission feature during the Metropolitan Opera's Saturday matinee broadcasts, three expert panelists were asked to name an opera with a saint in it. The panel was stumped at first. Then one person recalled Tchaikovsky's opera about Saint Joan. Another offered Messiaen's opera about Saint Francis. Finally, a panelist, straddling and stretching the question, suggested Liszt's oratorio on Saint Elizabeth and an obscure work about Saint Cecilia by a turn-of-the-century Vatican-sanctioned hack, Licinio Refice. No one thought of *Four Saints in Three Acts.*

Given the exhaustive musical knowledge possessed by most of the Texaco panelists, I have no doubt that they could have given key details of the plot of every stillborn American opera ever written, from Deems Taylor's *The King's Henchman* (libretto by Edna St. Vincent Millay) and Howard Hanson's *Merry Mount* to Roger Sessions's *Montezuma,* Aaron Copland's *The Tender Land,* and Samuel Barber's *Vanessa.* But no one recalled *Four Saints.* This, however, is just one side of the picture. Although the name of Virgil Thomson is most associated with something called "simplicity" in music, a quality he always brandished against the mostly Austro-German "complexity boys," Mr. Tommasini's biographical investigations also reveal a positive side to the still-accumulating ledger of ups and downs in Thomson's reputation. Here we must consider the testimony of Philip Glass, the famous—and at times reviled—author of *Einstein on the Beach.* Thomson, Mr. Glass noted, was

the godfather of experimental opera. Virgil was the maverick. He knew that the mode and style of operatic presentation, the content, the form—all these had to be renovated. When I started working with Robert Wilson, Virgil was the only person we had as a model.

The Stein-Thomson opera—striking, too, for its all-black ensemble—did recast the possibility for American opera well away from the European mold. As Mabel Dodge Luhan predicted at the time, "*Four Saints in Three Acts* would destroy opera the way Picasso has destroyed old painting!*"

The wording may have been exorbitant, but surely the melodramatic formulae of "grand" opera—whether it be Wagner, Meyerbeer, Saint-Saëns, Auber, even the Strauss-Hofmannsthal collaborations—all of them were just waiting for a fall. The genial nonsense, the alliterative play of Gertrude Stein gave Thomson the vehicle for his abstractive musical elaboration, as in St. Ignatius's ecstatic "If a magpie in the sky on the sky cannot cry if the pigeon on the grass alas can alas and to pass the pigeon on the grass alas. . . ." This was the start of the Thomsonian agenda—an admixture of his renowned "anti-complexity" bias, his fascination with Dada, his instinctive reaction against technical virtuosity in orchestration, even his own limitations as a composer and craftsman. Mr. Tommasini's study is the critical yet still fervent documentation of how that agenda got put into practice.

Thomson's musical aesthetic started on its wayward and quirky course early, when he was an apprentice pianist and organist in his native Kansas City. It continued throughout his years as an undergraduate music major at Harvard, where his music professor gave him a good rap across the knuckles in his senior year: "your work in the examination was of not sufficient merit . . . that you could be recommended for the degree with distinction, although you passed the examination. But your work was so mediocre in harmony, counterpoint and fugue that on the evidence submitted no other verdict was possible."

Thomson did excel as accompanist to the Harvard Glee Club for their European tour of 1921, a trip that brought him a fellowship to Paris, the world of "Les Six," and the tutelage of Nadia Boulanger. Although Thomson was always a Satie fanatic and Gallophile, the hidden ghost behind his harmonic plainness is the music of Charles Ives—not the massive tone clusters of the "Concord" Sonata or the more raucous moments of *Three Places in New England*, but the simpler and more evocative pages. This was the "simple" Ives that was precisely the aspect of his own music which most irritated Ives himself in his old age ("God damn simplicity," he once shouted to John Kirkpatrick).

It is good to remember that Ives, twenty-two years older than Thomson, had pretty much swept "the courtly muses of Europe" from his musical vocabulary, as his contentious battles with his German-trained mentor at Yale, Horatio Parker, demonstrated. Parker had called the young Ives's experiments in polytonality "hogging all the keys at one meal," and was all the more repelled by Ives's easy acceptance of Antonin Dvořák's suggestions to young American composers of the time that the use of hymn tunes and folk music of all sorts might serve as the beginnings of a national music. Ives certainly did make rich use of all the materials from popular musical culture that his bandmaster father had laid on the son. His early symphonies do have a gratefully Dvořákian echo— *The New World Symphony* having been written just one year before Ives took up his studies at Yale.

The influence of Ives on Thomson is a minor matter to Mr. Tommasini, since he has so many other fish to fry, but it is useful to place Ives as one of the prime makers of Thomson's way with sound. Thomson wrote a ruminative and well-pondered essay on Ives now collected in *A Virgil Thomson Reader*, and toward the end of his life he did simply state that Ives was "the father of us all," referring to the "Commando Squad" of young American composers who first came to prominence in the Thirties—Aaron Copland, Roy Harris, Walter Piston, Elie Siegmeister, and Bernard Herrmann among so many others. These are the composers who are rather archly described by Ives's biographer as the "milder moderns," some of whom were encouraged and performed by Serge Koussevitsky and the Boston Symphony Orchestra.

There may be a more obvious motive for Thomson's careful distance from Ives even during the life of the older composer. Virgil Thomson was a homosexual from way back to his Kansas City youth, and it is not something he at all wished on himself. "I didn't want to be queer," Thomson said in an interview. "No! No! No! That was another hurdle I didn't want to have to jump over. Nowadays it's much easier." Charles Ives was a homophobe of uncommon verbal spleen. As Ives's biographer notes, "Violence and panic exactly describe Ives's response to the specter of homosexuality, which was part of a fear of feminization even more threatening to him than to most artists of his time."

Thomson had to grow up with the kind of opprobrium that Ives and his generation handed out to homosexuals in the arts, and he was, furthermore, well aware of how icily Ives had treated his own disciple and future biographer, Henry Cowell, after Cowell had been convicted for homosexual activities and sent to San Quentin for four years. Mr. Tommasini had the privilege of getting to know Thomson when he was in old age and well-ensconced in the Chelsea Hotel, and is able to bring to his critical scrutiny a post-Stonewall frankness regarding an inner drama within Thomson that the very reticent subject never would himself have had the nerve or bravura to divulge: "Thomson would not allow his sexuality to be referred to in print. In his 420-page autobiography there is no mention of it, though there are veiled, mostly contrived stories of youthful attachments to women." Thomson disliked the term "gay" and was adamantly opposed to the glaring publicity which accompanied the gay liberation movement. He came perilously close to Cowell's fate, since he was picked up in a Brooklyn male brothel in 1942 (along with a sixty-nine-year-old Irish senator from Boston, by the way). This incident, retold in its entirety in Chapter 20, could have irreparably damaged Thomson as an artist and finished him definitively at *The New York Herald Tribune*; the matter was artfully managed somehow, though the owner of the Brooklyn operation spent twenty years in Sing

Sing. His sexuality is a constant threat and shadow over Thomson from the very beginning. Mr. Tommasini notes that even in Thomson's high-school yearbook, "his graduation photograph was captioned, 'O Shades of Oscar Wilde, Millet and Paderewski.' This may have amused the student editors, but the barb could have been no laughing matter to Thomson."

The stories and the gossip embedded in this study should not divert anyone from the larger issues that Thomson's musical and critical career represent. One thing is the Virgilian agenda, clearly under way in France under the tutelage of Nadia Boulanger, and very much audible in the opera and the orchestral suites from the Thirties. The style with which this same agenda is promulgated is directly related to its content, and this means vamping well beyond college days. Here is Thomson at twenty-six, recommending a demeanor for possible and future patrons: "Whenever I go to call on a middle-aged or elderly person of either sex, but particularly men, I do my complexion with cold cream and hot water, I run all the way up the stairs, and then slap myself as I ring the bell. Talk well, of course; put over your line, or whatever the cue is. But look your most adolescent."

A portrait emerges, not especially flattering. Thomson was obviously *prépotente*, supremely self-assured from the public point of view, very vain, very *mondain*, someone who evinced only rarely a sense of self-doubt or spiritual torment, a bully. He was not about to parcel out to the world any more of himself than he cared to reveal, and as Mr. Tommasini so carefully indicates, the closet life of Thomson well into his maturity and even old age required his fanatic supervision among all friends concerning what people were saying about him.

Nowhere in this study is there a kind of summing up, a pondered overview of the whole of Thomson's achievement, but an audition of the many recordings gives the sense that he was not at all comfortable or fluent in purely orchestral composition. When his sometimes fellow critic on the *Tribune*, Paul Bowles, reviewed a Thomson symphony and found it "awkward, droll and rough, but it is not static," that sounds about right. On the other hand, an attentive hearing of the two Stein-Thomson collaborations reveals once again their mastery of surprising rhythms, the joyful tension and release gained by inventive and ever-changing patterns of lengths and stress. Thomson represented, as did Kurt Weill, a happy apostasy within both the European and American avant-garde. He was so full of the remembered music of his youth—hymns, dances, parlor songs, negro gospel, waltzes, and two-steps—that the Schoenbergian revolution never really appealed to his ear. Though Thomson will forever rail against the "German-Austrian musical complex" in articles and interviews, I am not at all sure that Mr. Tommasini has done justice to Thomson's individual responses, in specific cases, to composers who did not at all jibe with the agenda. For instance, *A Virgil Thomson Reader* contains meticulous and admiring accounts of two works by Arnold Schoenberg—the Piano Concerto and the *Five Pieces for Orchestra*. The same for Alban Berg's Violin Concerto and Anton Webern's Symphony.

Mr. Tommasini is at his most trenchant when he observes and analyzes the glaring conflict of interest between a composer with performance ambitions acting as a music critic with an agenda. In this regard, he is not above a good zinger on the matter: "To no one's surprise but his own, performances of his works by top-name artists and orchestras dropped off after he left the *Herald Tribune*, and invitations to conduct declined." When the composer Peggy Glanville-Hicks approached Thomson about her replacing him on the paper early on in 1954, suggesting that "being the chief critic of so influential a paper would no doubt be a boon to her own career as a composer, Thomson grinned, looked her in the eye, and said, 'Baby! I've sucked that lemon dry.'"

For personal and artistic reasons, paranoia was never far from Thomson's spiritual state, but there is one anecdote in this study that must have given him every reason to feel like an oppressed minority in more than one sense. A fellow composer and student of Nadia Boulanger, Theodore Chanler, wrote a savage review of *Four Saints in Three Acts* for the then influential *Modern Music*, edited by Minna Lederman. Thomson was hurt and baffled by the review but let it pass. A decade later, when an early biographer of Thomson requested from Chanler a more detailed commentary on the review, he confessed that he really loved *Four Saints*, had been "much moved" by it, but had been hectored and browbeaten into writing a negative review of the work by the formidable and very dour symphonist Roger Sessions, "who simply pulverized me with scorn and indignation at having dared to like it." The fact that someone of the stature of Roger Sessions could lower himself to practice such conformist cultural Stalinism does give pause. This whole matter—the tyranny of the avant-garde in certain crucial moments of American cultural history—deserves a lot more treatment than Mr. Tommasini is willing to give it. And, too, the nasty commentary on the audiences at *Four Saints* by such luminaries as Olin Downes and Wallace Stevens makes Thomson's golden rule all the more urgent: "Never review the audience."

Virgil Thomson did survive to the state of an aged eminence, with honors at the Kennedy Center among other events. When, at the end of his life, he totted up the royalty payments he had received over the years for *The Mother of Us All*, he found that over one thousand separate productions had taken place, in colleges, amateur groups, or small opera companies. Having hammered a few nails into the set of *The Mother of Us All* when it was produced in Sanders Theatre at Harvard in the mid-Fifties, I can vouch for its total theatricality, the bite and the charm of it.

September 1997

Sviatoslav Richter, 1915–1997

THE RUSSIAN PIANIST Sviatoslav Richter died in his *dacha* outside Moscow on August 1, 1997. No one could ever have thought of this peerless artist as a dissident within his own country in the manner of Solzhenitsyn or Mstislav Rostropovich. Neither could one think of him or his wildly individualistic behavior during the darkest days of Stalin as anything but a special example of how art could triumph over the most crushing of political repressions. He earned his unparalleled personal freedom within the cultural politics of the Soviet system all right, but at a price— no visas for concerts abroad were allowed until 1959, when he was permitted a short tour of Finland. A debut at Carnegie Hall and an American tour began what was to be a regime of off-and-on summer exiles in France, Italy, and Germany, though he was still most assiduous in giving concerts to his countrymen in remotest Eastern Russia during whirlwind tours, since he felt that they were the people who needed music the most.

A good example of Richter's determination can be

found when we observe him playing at Stalin's funeral in 1953, an occasion where many Soviet artists were ordered to perform in memory of the great man. Richter was to play a short piece, appropriately lugubrious. Instead, he chose one of the longer and more elaborate preludes and fugues from Bach's *Well-Tempered Clavier*. In spite of repeated remonstrations that he had gone beyond the allotted time, Richter finished the particular prelude and fugue in the time needed to perform it. When he finished, he was roughly thrown out of the hall. He said that he could have been shot right then and there, but Khrushchev, Malenkov, and Bulganin were too busy struggling for power to be bothered about a "demented" pianist. He also played on an upright piano at Pasternak's funeral in 1960.

In spite of his Germanic family name, Richter was Russian through and through, an ardent Muscovite who was at the very least patriotic if not chauvinistic. He had no interest in "fleeing" to the West on a permanent basis. For both political and personal reasons, he rarely played any Stravinsky, and refused to meet or play with Rostropovich after the latter's triumphal return to Moscow from exile, though they had been long-standing musical partners in the old days. He was born in Zhitomir, Ukraine, the same birthplace as the great operatic basso Alexander Kipnis, born 1891. While someone of Kipnis's generation could make appearances at Berlin, Bayreuth, Glyndebourne, and the Metropolitan Opera, an artist of Richter's generation, born more or less with the Revolution, had harder luck. Richter's father was an organist and instilled some musical culture in his son, but he gave him no rudimentary lessons; the young Sviatoslav seems to have been essentially self-taught.

By the late Thirties, a family name such as Richter was not a good one to have in Stalinist Russia, before or after the Hitler-Stalin pact. Richter's mother, a distant descendant of Jenny Lind, used to insist that the family was of a lineage composed of "Russian, German, Polish, Swedish and Hungarian" forebears. At any rate, in an NKVD roundup ordered by the then chief of secret police Lavrenti Beria, seeking out all males with "German-sounding" names, Richter's father was arrested and summarily executed. His mother then married the younger brother of her late husband, and, after a series of frightful vicissitudes, found a home in West Germany. After Richter began his American tour in 1960, distant relatives organized a reunion between mother and son in Flushing, Queens, of all places. The fate of the mother was discovered by the American music critic Paul Moor, who was the first person to inform Richter that his mother was alive and well in West Germany.

While he was still in his early teens, his mother took him to the Odessa Conservatory, where he took his first formal lessons. Odessa was a hothouse of talent at that time—among Richter's colleagues from his student days were Rostropovich, Emil Gilels, and David Oistrakh. Richter was a natural, as they say— he never underwent the torture of a forced practice regime, the scales in all keys, the dreary Hanon and the hateful Czerny. He had monstrous hands. He could fit an octave between his index and little finger, while his full hand could easily encompass a twelfth, that is, an octave plus four notes. Still, he really had little serious intention of being a virtuoso pianist, since opera conducting and singers' accompanist were his early goals. He became proficient at sight-reading full orchestral and opera scores; in house concerts or simply for his own growing repertory, he read through at the piano all of the symphonies of Mahler and Tchaikovsky, all of Wagner and most of Strauss, and Debussy's *Pelléas et Mélisande*. This pianistic reduction of operatic and orchestral repertory is a fundamental key to an interpretation of Richter's mature playing—he veered away from the purely virtuoso style represented by Vladimir Horowitz to a more orchestrally voiced approach. Richter gave a debut recital in Odessa in 1934, then went to study at the Moscow Conservatory under the renowned teacher Heinrich Neuhaus, who became a spiritual father to Richter. In the fullness of time, Neuhaus would allege that "he hadn't taught Richter a thing," and that the young man had come to him already fully formed. This couldn't possibly be true; perhaps Neuhaus's tutelage had something to do with Richter's idiosyncratic view of the piano repertory in general. For instance, having heard his teacher in a performance of Beethoven's Piano Concerto No. 5, Richter swore that such a performance could never be equaled. Indeed, he never played it under any circumstances throughout his long career. He never played the popular Piano Concerto No. 4 of Beethoven, either, nor the "Moonlight" Sonata, not the immensely popular Piano Concerto No. 3 of Sergei Rachmaninoff. He would perform only particular works of any composer, and steadfastly refused to record the "complete" piano music of anyone, deeming it an idiocy fed by commercialism. Except for his friend Sergei Prokofiev's arrangements of some of his own orchestral ballets for piano, Richter never played adaptations or transcriptions.

Richter's brooding and unpredictable personality flowed directly in his approach into the piano. There was also a manic side to him that he freely admitted to the rare interviewer. His friend the young Russian pianist André Gavrilov swears that in his hearing, Richter repeated one page of a sonata some seventy times, while one bar might merit one or two hours. On other occasions, he would simply abandon the piano and not touch it for as long as five months. He took a great interest in a number of the other fine arts. More than proficient as a visual artist, he often let the piano go in order to sketch and to paint. His well-appointed Moscow apartment and his *dacha* were full of icons and contemporary European paintings from the Impressionists on, and he often said that he preferred the conversation and company of painters well over that of musicians. As he said, "I am an omnivorous creature and I want a lot of things."

Richter was physically stocky, with an oddly pugnacious stage presence. The psychologist Allen Wheelis, observing Richter at a concert, gave some idea of the peculiar atmosphere of a Richter recital, with the evident disconnection between the existence of a listening public and the intensity of concentration on what he was doing. Here is Wheelis's account as quoted in David Dubal's *The Art of the Piano*:

> Sviatoslav Richter strides out on the stage. His face is grim; there is anger in the set of his jaw, but not at the audience. This is a passion altogether his own, a force with which he protects what he is about to do. If it had words, it would say, "What I attempt is important and I go about it with utmost seriousness. I intend to create beauty and meaning, and everything everywhere threatens this endeavor: The coughs, the late-comers, the chatting women in the third row, and always those dangers within, distraction, confusion, loss of memory, weakness of hand, all are enemies of my endeavor. I call up this passion to oppose them, to protect my purpose." Now he begins to play, and the anger I see in his bearing I hear in the voice of Beethoven. It knows nothing of meanness or spite; it is the passion of the doer who will not let his work be swept aside. It hurts no one, it asserts life, it is the force that generates form.

Thanks to "live" recording, we have evidence of Richter's concentration during the most trying of circumstances—almost a laboratory demonstration of this capability within him, if you will. It occurred at the infamous Richter recital given in Sofia, Bulgaria, in 1958, and now newly reissued on a Philips CD. The program was par for the course, that is, for Richter. He *opened* the program with the very daunting *Pictures at an Exhibition*, of Modest Mussorgsky, in its original version for piano. After the intermission, he played works of Schubert, Chopin, and Liszt. What makes these performances unusual is the physical condition of the audience: Sofia was plagued by a flu epidemic, and the coughing during the performance of *Pictures* is well nigh unbearable. As the work progresses, one senses Richter driving himself inward. The more they cough, it would seem, the more demonic and unsettling the performance. This recording, along with his hypnotic Schumann recital on Deutsche Grammophon (above all the *Forest Scenes* and the *Fantasy Pieces*), might be a good place to start a new generation listening to Richter's art. He was a great pianist, of course, but he was also beyond category, or, as *Le Monde* put it, "Richter was unique because he was a bit crazy and a bit of an idealist."

October 1997

City Opera; Stuyvesant Park

T HE STATUS of City Opera as New York's "second" opera company does not necessarily imply
that the "first" opera house, the Metropolitan, is performing impeccably, or indeed is giving the most
responsible account of the full operatic repertory,
from baroque to contemporary. The Met, like Homer,
can and does nod.

The opening weeks of the fall season of eight
productions at the "new" New York City Opera
represent the first productions presented under the
leadership of general and artistic director Paul Kellogg, appointed in January 1996 to succeed the late
Christopher Keene. Mr. Kellogg was the founder and
nurturer of the Glimmerglass Opera in Cooperstown,
New York, since 1979, a unique experimental summer opera festival that has featured both new and
traditional works. One naturally hopes that Mr. Kellogg's arrival will bring new life to an opera company
that, since its founding in the mid-1940s, has become
an organic part of New York cultural life. Among
other things, City Opera has come to be a useful

counterpoise to its gargantuan neighbor at Lincoln Center. Following the past innovations of Julius Rudel, Beverly Sills, Christopher Keene, and now Mr. Kellogg, the company projects a fall and spring schedule of freshened oldies and new and revived works—operas of Tan Dun and Tobias Picker along with a resuscitation of Britten's *Paul Bunyan*, libretto by W. H. Auden, an early fruit of Britten and Auden's dalliance in the early Forties with life in the United States.

Going back a few years, one remembers that this company, in spite of whatever the vicissitudes it has suffered over the past decades, has functioned as a critical goad and contrast to the Met, performing Berg's *Wozzeck* in 1959 and pioneering fluent performances of the operas of Handel and Monteverdi, which were not often performed across the plaza. City Opera has encouraged contemporary American works (such as the now temporarily postponed *Esther* of Hugo Weisgall) and, in general, has been more daring even in the presentation of warhorses from the repertory. Two of their recent productions immediately come to mind—the extraordinary *Die Soldaten* of Bernd Alois Zimmermann (Fall 1991) and the more recent *Mathis der Maler* of Paul Hindemith (Fall 1995). The latter production (a performance splendidly conducted by Robert Duerr, replacing the ailing Christopher Keene) did dramatize, however, certain limitations in past productions by the company. Having seen prior stagings of *Mathis der Maler* in Boston and Vienna, under the respective musical direction of Sarah Caldwell and Karl Böhm, this reviewer can attest that the New York production was by far the most impressive musical realization of the work. The deficiencies were visual. One would hardly have been able to glean, except for the presence of the inevitable easel, that Matthias Grünewald was, with his *Isenheim Altarpiece* of 1515, a visionary painter of phantasmagoria equal to those of his near-contemporary Hieronymus Bosch. To this end, Ms. Caldwell had spread magnified patches of the most lurid parts of the triptych, projecting them onto scrims all over the otherwise rudimentary Boston staging; the effect was unsettling. The singers seemed haunted by the constant presence of Grünewald's art. Almost in spite of itself, Hindemith's heavy-handed allegory about the conflicts between politics and art came alive. In the New York City Opera production, it wasn't really a question of lack of financial resources, but an evident lack of imagination, something that Sarah Caldwell possessed in her heyday and which, some early notices have suggested, Mr. Kellogg is displaying these days.

For a start, it might be instructive to see how this company is performing two classic works from the repertory: Mozart's *Magic Flute* and a work still on the fringe of acceptance, Verdi's *Macbeth*. In the excellent English translation of Andrew Porter, City Opera's *Magic Flute* (in and out of production since its premiere a decade ago) was sung by a cast quite different from that of opening night earlier in September—a good test of vocal depth for any company. In general, the opera came across winningly and with proper brio under the baton of Derrick Inouye. The success of this production is all the more impressive given the wild tonal mixtures inherent in this "simple" but intractable opera, ranging from the proto-vaudeville comic jesting of the bumpkin Papageno, on to the stern and earnest Tamino and Pamina, then the "secular awe, without churchliness" (the words of musicologist Alfred Einstein) emanating from Sarastro's sublime arias.

Futile as it is to complain about the acoustics and the space at the New York State Theater, it may still be the case that this opera ideally prospers only in more limited theatrical venues, such as the eighteenth-century Swedish house used by Ingmar Bergman in his film of the opera, or indeed—even more minimally—as enchantingly projected by the Salzburger Marionette Theater. Nonetheless, Thierry Bosquet's sets and costumes, imposing in the temple scenes and appropriately bosky for Papageno, Tamino, and Pamina, exude the fairy-tale atmosphere so essential to draw an audience—and New Yorkers above all—into the particular world of *The Magic Flute*. The acting and the voice-production of Richard Clement as Tamino and Amy Burton as Pamina were engaging and fresh, and one can have only good things to say about the bumptious characterization of Papageno by Stephen Powell and the especially nasty and unctuous Monostatos of Jonathan Green. If the roles of the Queen of the Night and Sarastro—one in the musical stratosphere, the other descending to Plutonian depths—were not realized with absolute ease, the attainment of the near-impossible has to be more than sufficient for the purposes at hand. The dancing animals, tamed and subdued by Tamino's calming flute, were charmingly choreographed by Jessica Redel. The only disappointment was the plastic and highly unthreatening dragon attacking Tamino at the beginning of the opera—more writhing and snarling are in order. The three ladies, vigorous singers that they are, had their long forks at the ready, but stayed at such a distance from the thing that it seemed to expire on its own.

Verdi's *Macbeth* is not exactly a staple of any opera company in the way that the composer's *Otello* and *Falstaff* most certainly are. This relatively early work, which the Verdi critic Julian Budden ranked "with *Nabucco*, *Ernani*, and *Luisa Miller* as one of the four undisputed repertory pieces of the pre-*Rigoletto* period," was first performed in Florence in 1847 and in a revised version for Paris in 1865. The opera received an inordinate amount of affection from Verdi himself, who continued to be irritated and baffled by the fact that it was never popular even among Verdians. As Michael Feingold suggested in his program notes, "Giuseppe Verdi never knew what any English or American actor of the mid-nineteenth century—or our own time, for that matter—could have told him: Shakespeare's *Macbeth* is a play with a curse on it." Verdi's version was not premiered in New York for ninety-two years after the Paris performances. It was the New York City Opera which gave *Macbeth* its first hearing, in 1957. The following year, the

Metropolitan Opera took it up as a vehicle for the stellar baritone Leonard Warren, and it was this version that was recorded for RCA Victor under the baton of Erich Leinsdorf.

Leaving aside the generalized hex surrounding anything to do with the Scottish Play, there are fairly cogent reasons for the lack of enthusiasm for the opera over the years. It is, as the Italian critics would have it, the "opera senza amore," a work without a compelling love interest since, differing from the Shakespearean original, Verdi's librettist has turned Lady Macbeth into an all-consuming, driving harridan who is at the source of all Macbeth's actions, while in the original play the murder of Banquo is "something that Macbeth deliberately keeps from his wife," as Budden has noted. In short, there is little passion in the opera, and this is further complicated by the fact that there is a glaring absence of a star role for a romantic tenor. Macduff's aria in the last act, impressive as it is in the lament for his massacred children, comes way too late for the expectations of most opera lovers, desirous as they are of a ringing set of tenor arias scattered throughout. Some of the martial music is pedestrian, to say the least. On the other hand, a compelling sleepwalker's scene by "the Lady" (as Verdi referred to her), the apparition scenes, and the general mischief as predicted by the witches all make for a well-crafted operatic melodrama, despite one sniping critic's appraisal of the weird sisters: "Verdi's witches, like Shakespeare's, are out of St. Trinian's." Question: how did the cartoons of Ronald

Searle get into the making of *Macbeth*? Oh, well; as T. S. Eliot said, the new always creates its own precursors.

For this production, the only entirely new effort this fall, John Conklin has devised an appropriately grim Erector set of girders, a crane, and industrial stairwells, with costumes drab enough for Scotland, its soldiers and exiles. Leon Major, the director, has made the best use possible of the space designed originally, let us not forget, for Balanchine and the New York City Ballet. Verdi, in a letter to an impresario about a future production of the opera, insisted that "you will see that I need an excellent chorus: especially the female chorus must be good because there will be two witch choruses of the greatest importance. Pay attention also to the stage-machinery. In short, the things that require the greatest care in this opera are: *Chorus and Machinery*." Under the music direction of George Monahan, the orchestra and chorus were in lusty and supple coordination with each other, in spite of the varied distances between the pit, principals, and chorus. Apparitions and ghosts were well done.

It is true that there were a few torpid moments in the direction of stage business. In the culminating assassination of Banquo in Act Two, for example, Macbeth's henchmen are ordered to do away with Fleance at the same time they finish off his father, Banquo. In this production, however, as the daggers are plunged into Banquo, the murderers practically do curtsies for Fleance and make way for the child's escape; he saun-

ters off into the wings instead of being the object of a
hot pursuit across the stage as Verdi wanted. On the
other hand, the slow-motion battle between Birnam
Wood and Dunsinane during the orchestral fugue in
the last act is splendidly staged. Mark Delavan's
portraiture of Macbeth could use a good dose of
malevolent *terribilità*, so laid-back and round-toned is
he, while "the Lady," as sung hell-for-leather by
Lauren Flanigan, was balefully just right.

STUYVESANT PARK, located just above Fourteenth
Street at Second Avenue, must be one of the most ig-
nored of pleasant places in downtown New York City.
On December 13, 1941, Mayor LaGuardia, accom-
panied by various eminences, including Jan Masaryk,
Bruno Walter, and Fritz Kreisler, dedicated a plaque
affixed to the brownstone at 327 East Seventeenth
Street, facing the park, where the Czech composer
Antonín Dvořák had lived for nearly three years as
director of the National Conservatory of Music of
America, the only school of the arts ever blessed with
a congressional charter from both House and Senate.
Mayor LaGuardia declared Dvořák's home a "land-
mark," and there was talk of a museum. Some fifty
years later, in August 1991, the building was
demolished to make way for an AIDS treatment center.
   Another ignominy had preceded the event of August
1991. A fine bronze statue of Dvořák a bit more than
life-size, the last work of the Croatian-American
sculptor Ivan Meštrović (1883–1962), had been do-
nated in 1963 to the New York Philharmonic by the

Czechoslovak National Council of America. The management of the orchestra responded to this largesse by relegating the work to the roof of Avery Fisher Hall, invisible to the public, where over the years it suffered severe pitting and general deterioration.

Thanks to the efforts of Mr. Steven Richman, the music director and conductor of the Harmonie Ensemble/ New York and founding member of the Dvořák American Heritage Association, the statue has been rescued from the roof of the concert hall, newly conserved and refinished, mounted on a splendid green granite pedestal, and placed in front of what was Dvořák's home, just at the northeast corner of Stuyvesant Park. This brings us to "Dvořák's Day," September 13, 1997, the unveiling of the restored statue.

In a ceremony presided over by Henry J. Stern, the commissioner of parks and recreation, a full complement of speakers attested to the significance of the event. Indeed, Mr. Jack Taylor, the head of the Stuyvesant Park Neighborhood Association, spoke in bitterly exorbitant terms of the lost fight for the preservation of the home in the years prior to 1991, while more celebratory comments were given by the Czech-born film director Milos Forman; the Czech ambassador to the United States, Alexandr Vondra; the mayor of Prague, Jan Koukal; and the first lady of the City of New York, Donna Hanover.

Mr. Richman must have been aware that the music was the thing—the music written by Dvořák both in New York City and in Spillville, Iowa, where he spent an intervening summer in a Czech émigré farmer community. Following the dedication of the statue, a concert of Dvořák's music was given at St. George's Church at the western edge of Stuyvesant Square, where up to the time of Dvořák's attendance the most famous parishioner had been J. P. Morgan. Greetings were read by Vaclav Havel and by Antonín Dvořák III, a bald and portly gentleman who had the air of good cheer that Dvořák's music always seems to exude. The concert began with the participation of the Czech violinist Josef Suk, another great-grandson of Dvořák, playing the Sonatina for Violin and Piano along with the Humoresque in G-flat major, done briskly and forthrightly, without a touch of sentimentality. Mr. Suk, joined by two members of the Guarnieri Quartet, Michael Tree and Arnold Steinhardt, then played the attractive *Terzetto* for String Trio. After the intermission, Mr. Richman, with a full orchestra composed of instrumentalists drawn from every major orchestra in the city, directed a rousing performance of the symphony *From the New World*, with the English horn solo in the Largo played exquisitely by Iveta Bachmannová of the Prague Symphony Orchestra.

November 1997

Alicia de Larrocha
at Carnegie Hall

THE RISE of the virtuoso pianist during the Romantic period led to a serious decline in the public's appreciation of quiet musicianship. As a result, so much of the best music from the nineteenth century and earlier did not appeal to audiences, who had come to expect the cannonading and empty pyrotechnics of the worst (though often the most admired) demonstrative virtuosos. It was a problem that persisted well into this century in the playing of Ignace Paderewski and Josef Hofmann, and culminated in the highly charged performances of Vladimir Horowitz.

There is an anecdote from César Saerchinger's biography *Artur Schnabel* (1957) that illustrates the difference between mere virtuosity and genuine musicianship. After the eleven-year-old Schnabel began studying with the famed Viennese pedagogue Theodor Leschetitzky in 1893, the teacher quickly took stock of the pupil and uttered a judgment that was also an admonition: "Artur," he intoned, "you will never be a pianist. *You* are a musician." To that end, Leschetitzky forbade his student such works as the *Hungarian Rhapsodies* of Franz Liszt, and instead directed his attentions to piano works by Schubert, then lying in oblivion—"Schubert has written fifteen sonatas for piano which almost nobody knows. They are absolutely forgotten. No one ever plays them. *You* might like them." Of course, it was Schnabel's later recordings of Schubert's impromptus, *Moments Musicaux*, and many of the sonatas that brought these works back into the musical repertory.

The instructive distinction between a mere pianist and a musician was very much on my mind as I attended the piano recital by Alicia de Larrocha at Carnegie Hall in March.* As befitted this esteemed artist, now in her seventy-fifth year, this was very much a celebratory occasion. De Larrocha began her career as an exacting but undemonstrative musician at the age of five with a private recital in her native Barcelona, where her small audience was composed of some friends of her teacher Frank Marshall, including the composer Joaquín Turina. Her first public performance, in Madrid at age eleven, was of Mozart's "Coronation" concerto. A distinguished mainstay of the Mostly Mozart summer concerts for more than three decades, de Larrocha has produced a splendid legacy of recordings both of classic works from Bach onward and of—her specialty—the music of Spain.

Given de Larrocha's impressive musical accomp-

---

* Alicia de Larrocha performed works by Frédéric Chopin, Joaquín Turina, and Isaac Albéniz at Carnegie Hall, New York, on March 27, 1998.

lishments, I naturally went to the Carnegie Hall recital with high expectations. They were not, regrettably, entirely fulfilled. First of all, there was the matter of the program itself—four works of Chopin, at least two of them masterpieces of their kind, which altogether added up to some thirty-five minutes of music. Then, after what seemed to be an interminable intermission, there were dances by Joaquín Turina and two relatively short works of Isaac Albéniz that were played perfunctorily. Perhaps it is churlish to complain of being musically short-changed, but the lack of breadth and general weight in this recital left me with a sense of disappointment, especially given the catholic nature of de Larrocha's musical interests.

As for her performance, all of the notes were of course securely in place, and the tonal sheen from the piano was a constant joy to hear, but the dynamics were so carefully modulated that nary a true forte was heard throughout the evening, not to mention anything resembling a fortissimo. On the plus side, it can be said that this delicate approach to the keyboard commanded the undivided attention of the listener: it drew you in. Still, there were moments—in the Chopin *Barcarolle* and the *Polonaise-fantasie* in particular—when more projection might have given the music a broader dynamic palette. I cannot recall a more uninflected, even underplayed, performance of the *Barcarolle*. Perhaps we have been corrupted by the excessive rubato and constant tempo variation of such pianists as Arthur Rubinstein and Ivan Moravec, two players for whom a nanosecond's delay in the delivery of a note or a chord and a constantly shifting pulse make all the difference in the final effect. Rather than evoking the Venetian gondola songs and the generally sumptuous Latin atmosphere intended by the composer, Miss de Larrocha's *Barcarolle* was a brisk, get-on-with-it traversal of the music: bracing enough on its own terms, but without much transport or charm.

Again, this was a recital by a *musician*, but one who now has taken self-effacement and sonic modesty too far. De Larrocha's attitude toward the music remained what it always has been—intensely devotional and chaste. Possibly (and with this I end my quibbles) the recital would have been more fortunately realized in a smaller, more intimate setting. In any event, the reception by the audience was notably fervent.

Perhaps I should now declare an interest. As a former professor of Spanish literature, I was always aware that among the constants of Spanish intellectual and cultural life in the twentieth century were not only the relation of contemporary artistic practice to its splendid historical legacy going back to the Spanish Golden Age and before, but also the question of how the culture of Spain relates to the rest of Europe. In political terms, the European Union may have given the answer, but in the nineteenth and twentieth centuries, and certainly after the catastrophe of the Spanish-American War of 1898, these were, to use a famous Spanish phrase, *cuestiones palpitantes*. As in Russia, there were advocates of a cultural identity for the country distinct from European values, while others saw the future only in the relation of Spain to the rest of Europe and of course to Spanish America.

In Barcelona and throughout Catalonia in general, the question becomes all the more complex, given Catalonia's distinct language, proximity to France, boisterous political orientations (severely repressed by Franco), and above all its cultural *renaxensa* in painting, architecture, and music well under way by the turn of the century. Madrid may have been the seat of the court and the central government, but Barcelona was more vibrant and forward-looking in all senses. In music, it was here that Pau (Pablo) Casals (1876–1973) played a decisive role in the establishment of basic standards for the performance of the symphonic repertory in Spain. Casals's Orquesta Pau Casals gave its first concerts in 1920, three years before the birth of Alicia de Larrocha, and continued for seventeen years in Barcelona and other cities in Spain until the onset of the Spanish Civil War and Casals's permanent exile abroad. The orchestra was initially funded almost entirely by concert fees earned abroad by the cellist himself, and it was he who conducted a considerable number of the concerts.

No orchestra in Spain could equal it: they made fine recordings (some Beethoven symphonies, the Brahms Double Concerto with the violinist Jacques Thibaud) and were directed by some sixty guest conductors over the seventeen-year life of the orchestra—including such distinguished figures as Otto Klemperer,

Serge Koussevitsky, Hermann Scherchen, Richard Strauss, Igor Stravinsky, and Anton Webern. A piquant aspect of Casals's fervent republicanism was the workers' concerts given by the orchestra, where the working public was admitted *only* if their income fell well below a modest top figure. How this was administered is anyone's guess, but the plain, drab clothing of the public at the first concert elated Casals. The point is that this was the hallowed musical standard that reigned in Barcelona until 1937— the performances were nonvirtuosic, with a studied lack of flamboyance. Simplicity and integrity in the delivery of the music were essential. These were the musical values espoused by Casals within Spain and later at the Prades and Perpignan Festivals after the Second World War, the Marlboro Festival in Vermont, and the Casals Festival in Puerto Rico. (For Casals's complete performance history, see H. L. Kirk's *Pablo Casals: A Biography* from 1974.) It seems clear that Casals's whole approach to music and performance had an immense impact on the developing years of Alicia de Larrocha.

A key problem confronting a budding instrumentalist born in Spain is the conflict between the demands of a career in Spain as a "Spanish" artist and those entailed by a career abroad. Casals himself, while a solid advocate of the music of Manuel de Falla, Enrique Granados, and other Spanish composers, centered his artistic achievement on major canonic European composers from Bach through Dvořák, Saint-Saëns, Elgar, and Bloch. In this sense, he was an internationally renowned artist who happened to hail from Vendrell, Catalonia.

Born forty-seven years after Casals, Alicia de Larrocha has made an equally determined effort to go beyond national boundaries. Though her mother and her aunt were students of the grand virtuoso composer Granados, it is a measure of de Larrocha's determinedly classical formation as a fledgling artist that she played no Spanish music at all (admittedly at the insistence of her teacher) until she was eighteen years old, that is, around 1941. The basic fare during these formative years was Bach, Scarlatti, Mozart, Beethoven, Chopin, and Debussy. The formation remained a constant with her—as one critic recently observed, "She prefers not to be known as a 'Spanish pianist,' but as a pianist who happens to be Spanish." This classicism has served her well over the years as she began to approach Spanish music, above all that of the late nineteenth and early twentieth centuries. As she sternly noted to the critic Raymond Ericson in 1966, "Spanish music is very very very hard. . . . if you cannot play Bach and Mozart well, you cannot play Spanish music well."

As for her interpretive models, she mentions two quite different pianists—the German pianist Wilhelm Kempff (1895–1991), an artist of singing tone and very measured tempi; and her friend and mentor Arthur Rubinstein (1887–1982), whose increasing affection for Spanish music after his first tour of Spain in 1916 led him to be known, among much else, as a proponent of Spanish piano music. Indeed, I can vouch for the fact that it was a rare Rubinstein concert that did not end (after many encores) with a blazing rendition of Falla's *Ritual Fire Dance.*

But the truth is that Rubinstein looked upon all of Spanish music as mere exotica. As he ruefully admitted to the critic Samuel Chotzinoff many years later,

> I must confess that, while I was happy to give pleasure with Spanish music, my heart really belonged more to the classics, old and new—to Bach, Mozart, Beethoven, Schubert, Schumann, Chopin, to the impressionists, to Debussy and Ravel and our Polish Szymanowski. I played Spanish music in such a way that my audiences found it hard to resist me. And that, my dear fellow, was a tragedy for me. . . . I gave people what they wanted in the way they wanted and I had a big success, but there was a void in my heart. Musically speaking, I was leading a double life.

What was a double life for the older pianist became a coalesced whole in the career of Alicia de Larrocha— her recorded performances of Albéniz, Falla, Granados, Turina, and Federic Mompou are treasured for their measured sobriety and their rhythmic sprightliness. But, at the same time, keep in mind that she has recorded all five Beethoven piano concerti, along with a rich sampling of Chopin, Schumann, Haydn, Mozart, Grieg, and Mendelssohn.

I bring up these matters only to suggest that, at this stage of her career, where her playing is ruminative and intimate, a rich program representing the true breadth of her repertory would have made for a more satisfying seventy-fifth-anniversary concert—much more Beethoven, Haydn, Schubert, Schumann, Franck, or Fauré.

May 1998

192

Part Three

Life in Basqueland

T HE DOUR CITY of Bilbao, located on the Basque
coast of Northeastern Spain on the Bay of Biscay,
has not exactly been an attraction for tourists to the
peninsula over the years—nothing, that is, compared
to the varied allure represented by Seville and Granada, or even Madrid and Barcelona. Something still
remains of Bilbao's rustbelt past; it is a city of some
400,000, renowned throughout Spain as a center for
banking, steel mills, shipping, and shipyards. As a
cultural force, it has always represented a liberal mer-
cantile counterpoise to the rural, conservative ten-
dencies of the Basque people.

The city survived three horrendous sieges by the
reactionary Carlist forces in the nineteenth century,
and it was almost razed to the ground by General
Francisco Franco, who viewed the short-lived Basque
autonomous government in Bilbao (permitted by the
republic) as a mortal threat to his future domination of
the nation, as it surely was. In *The Basque History of
the World* (Walker & Company), Mark Kurlansky's
overview of the Basque people, the city was spared this

time, because Franco's German advisors instead decided to pounce on the spiritual home of the Basque people, a town called Guernica, with a notorious massacre later made palpable to all by the hand of Pablo Picasso.

Bilbao is indirectly involved in a topic taken up by Kurlansky late in his book—the whys and wherefores of the construction of the new Guggenheim Museum designed by Frank Gehry. In this disenchanted scrutiny of the matter, Kurlansky notes that the town of San Sebastián, the cultural, if not the political, center of the Basques, was summarily dismissed as a prospective site for the museum. The unlikely winner, Bilbao, was chosen partly because it was the headquarters of the Basque Nationalist Party (known as the PNV), founded on July 31, 1895 (Ignatius de Loyola's saint's day) by the fiery racist ideologue Sabino Arana. The party and its minions in the Basque autonomous government, which governs the area within Spain, paid the $100 million tab for the construction of the museum, not to mention an additional fee paid to the New York museum "for using the Guggenheim name on the building." The greatest anomaly is that Basque art was and is to be the last of the new Museum's concerns; rather, "nation-building" and political outreach were the prime motives behind this utterly fantastic venture. Most important of all, the world-wide publicity accompanying the opening would make use of the denomination "Basque" without the usual accompanying "terrorist," and *that* was the heart of the matter, full stop.

As the head of the PNV gloated to reporters,

> It was expensive, but it was cheap for what we got. . . . It is a great thing for the future. More than we ever thought, it is an important building. Everyone recognizes that it is a great building, greater than what is in it.

As an avid aficionado of the fortunes of the Basque people and a researcher into their history in the Pyrenees over the past two or three thousand years, Kurlansky's study implicitly asks broader questions about the Basques, Spain, and the European Union. Thus a reader might ask: Does it make any sense now to try to make a nation out of what he calls "Basqueland" comprising four Spanish provinces and three French, all of 8,318 square miles, "slightly smaller than New Hampshire"? Moreover, is it valid to still work away at such a Basque utopia when Europe is moving in the opposite direction, that is, toward unification and the dissolving of frontiers? Isn't there some dreadful lesson to be learned about the drive toward "ethnic purity" from the fate of the remains of Yugoslavia? Don't these mindless massacres and wholly tragic migrations of what were former neighbors tell us far too much about how little justification there is for such activity, all while still keeping in mind the power of supposedly "ancestral" rights or how grievous the apparent victimization of a people in the distant or recent past? As is well known, the Basque people are divided by a national frontier.

Paris and Madrid have very fixed ideas about national unity, and the carving out of another nation from within these two geographical entities is not easily envisioned—except, that is, by a determined minority of very, very violent Basques.

The evidence of historians from Strabo and Plutarch on down reminds us that the Basques were a fiercely independent people speaking a strange language utterly unrelated to high or low Latin, or any of its local corruptions and variants amongst the Romance family. Successive invaders into the Pyrenees—Celts, Romans, Arabs, Visigoths—all quickly learned some brisk lessons about Basque ferocity and bravery. The Basques also gained the admiration of observers for their mode of self-government, their innate democratic leanings *avant la lettre*, and, in the Christian era, their sturdy piety and allegiance to the church.

The Basque people were a fundamental part of the triumph of the Spanish Empire in the old and new worlds, whether as soldiers, sailors, whalers, cod fishermen, shepherds, bankers, or iron forgers (Shakespeare's word for a fine sword is a "bilbo," from Bilbao, then a smithy center). They were indispensable to Columbus in his various exploits. Not to be overlooked is the fact that, in the days of heavily guarded frontiers, the Basque art of smuggling anything and everything made for a rich underground economy in the mountains. Basque names are all over Spanish America today, for they were avid colonialists. With the collapse of the Spanish empire in 1898, the particular linguistic groupings within peninsular Spain—Galician (Gallego), Catalonian (Catalan), Basque (Euskera/Vasco), among many others—asserted their identity against what they correctly sensed as an enfeebled central power in Madrid. The movement toward autonomy, now formalized in today's Spain, began in earnest—a centrifugal process observed by José Ortega y Gasset in his *Invertebrate Spain* (1921).

BUT THE GALICIANS and the Catalans are offshoots from Latin culture; they are newcomers on the peninsular block. The special uniqueness of the Basques is much heralded by Kurlansky, and he proffers a wealth of data to show that the Basque people, their genetic profile, and their language are indeed very special cases within the whole context of the historical development of Western Europe, and that they are not candidates for bland assimilation in the "hands across the borders" manner. Consider their language: Kurlansky mentions the fact that it is an agglutinative language, similar to Finnish and Hungarian, but he doesn't seem to be aware of the most recent determinations, namely, that Basque is a vestige of the language of the Aquitanian people, the last pre-Indo European language group to survive in the area extending from the Pyrenees to the Garonne and on down to present-day Navarre. These people were extant during the first millennium BC, that is, before Celtic or Latin linguistic interference. Aquitanian inscriptions and tombs in Latin letters from after the Roman invasions, and the common ancestry of ordinary nouns in Aquitanian and present-day Basque seem to bear this genealogy out.

Blood analyses tell much as well: 50 percent of the Basques have type "O" blood, the highest in the world; 27 percent have "O" Rh-negative, the highest in Europe. The inference is that the Basques, because of genetic isolation in their mountain fastness, descend right down from Cro-Magnon man, "there being no evidence for any change in population in the area for thousands of years before the arrival of the Celts and later the Romans in the first millennium BC."*

Kurlansky also describes a distinctive physical characteristic of the Basque people, something that most Spaniards outside of the Basque territories readily affirm. The version here given is that "there is a Basque type with a long straight nose, thick eyebrows, strong chin, and long earlobes," topped, it would seem, by the inevitable beret. This writer finds confirmation of this description in any photograph of the composer Maurice Ravel, born in Ciboure in French "Basqueland" just over the border—his is a classic Basque countenance.

Kurlansky has so much on his plate that some of the heavier ideological considerations determining the present political situation in the area get relatively short shrift. But speaking of plates, mention should be made of the splendid gastronomical aspect of this study. A good number of Basque specialities, available

---

* See Larry Trask's essential website on the Basques: www.cogs.susx.ac.uk/users/larryt/basque.html.

only in the region or in specifically Basque restaurants in major Spanish cities, have been here laid out within the fabric of Kurlansky's narrative. Notably and seemingly succulent as "virtual" dishes on the page are the "Espellete peppers and duck hearts," the "Pimientos de Guernica," the "Beans of Tolosa with cabbage and blood sausage garnish," and, most particularly, the "Hare with walnut and chocolate," a distant descendant of the chocolate *mole* brought back from Mexico by soldiers captained by Hernán Cortés. The pleasures of the table have a high place in Basque culture. It is gratifying and amusing to know that the mayor of San Sebastián in the province of Guipúzcoa is expected to eat at least once a year in each of the city's *seventy-five* gastronomical societies.

In darker tones, Kurlansky brings some insight into the motivation of the most violent of the Basque terrorist groups now active: the ETA. But Kurlansky is a valiant defender of the Basque cause, and his bias becomes too evident—he is an apologist for the autonomous ambitions of a certain sector of the Basque people, who are by no means a majority. Kurlansky could have said a lot more in a negative way and gone a lot deeper.

The recently published studies by Jon Juaristi, a Basque professor and formerly a jailed militant, demonstrate how, in an apparently "democratic" era where the secularization of the state is complete and where the Basques have achieved an almost complete autonomy in the federalist sense, violence—particularly a kind of sacralized violence—is still main-

201

tained by a fanatic minority as if it were a religion to live by. And this is a phenomenon deeply opposed by the Basque majority, who have been marching in the streets in the tens of thousands over the years to stop the madness.

Juaristi's criticisms, besides their savagery, also carry with them a high degree of humor. Recently, referring to a wholly autonomous Basque state sometime in the far future, he predicted that

> we'll become a theme park for the "live and direct" study of the roots of European Neolithic civilization. . . . I'll spend my time filling out questionnaires handed out by language inspectors . . . there will be cocktails at the Guggenheim.

These barbs have earned him the unenviable status of a near-persona non grata in the Basque country.

INDEED, one of the final ironies that Kurlansky couldn't possibly have been aware of is the fact that the Basque Nationalist Party head he quotes in his book, Xabier Arzalluz—the man who so fatuously boasted about the funding of the Guggenheim in Bilbao in all of its glory—is the same Arzalluz who, piqued after reading Juaristi's stinging critiques of Basque "autonomous" fantasies for the next millennium—descended to the level of repeatedly suggesting to Juaristi that "if he were not happy here, neighboring Castile is a broad and welcoming land." Such sinister suggestions of voluntary exile for a dissident in matters of cultural policy clearly signal the end of critical thinking in Basqueland, however constituted. And this would be so even if both sides of the Basque people were to retain their present status in Spain and France respectively, but with increasingly "indigenous" and "puristic" language pressures applied to all recalcitrants, in the manner now well ensconced in Québec.

Still, the PNV is an establishmentarian party, not really violent. The ETA, however, works through its own cliques and compartmentalized cells. Sensing pressures from the populace occasioned by the peace process in Northern Ireland, the ETA declared a "total, unilateral, indefinite, and unconditional truce" on September 16, 1998. After fruitless negotiations with Madrid, the hardliners in the ETA won out over the political wing, and the truce was broken on December 3, 1999, after fourteen months of relative civic peace. Just this past Christmas season, two truck bombs were intercepted by the civil guard on their way to Madrid, one containing 950 kilos of explosives, the other 750 kilos, three times more powerful than any of the previous twenty-six car or truck bombs endured by Madrid over the past decades. Both bombs were timed to go off at 7:56 P.M., just when offices were closing and the streets would be most congested. The minister of the interior called it a "Death Caravan." Mr. Arzalluz, infallible in his foolishness, congratulated the minister and his forces for having found the bombs, but alleged at the same time that "he would have been delighted if [they] had exploded," since it would have permitted more repression from Madrid against the Basque people.

At the end of this intriguing study of the fortunes of the Basque people over the past few thousand years, Kurlansky quotes an old and ultimately attractive Basque saying—"Let us be what we are." This is a crystalline formulation that contrasts mightily with the impossibility of the total "autonomous" realization of a Basque homeland in the larger contexts of the political structures of both Spain and France.

April 2000

¿O Plomo o Plata?

A LL NATIONS exhibit some degree of chauvinism, and embattled Mexico—"so far from God and so close to the United States" in the words of a distinguished ex-president—has certainly indulged in its share of nationalistic rhetoric and chest-pounding. But since the revolution in the early 1920s, Mexico has also opened out onto the world. It welcomed hundreds of thousands of refugees from the Spanish Civil War, and in general has pursued a cultural policy emphasizing the unity of Spanish-speaking peoples by means of prizes, symposia, invitations, and publishing houses that are open to all Spaniards and Spanish Americans. Just in the past year, for instance, the cultural arms of both the federal government and of Mexico City itself have been celebrating the hundredth anniversary of the birth of the Argentinian poet Jorge Luis Borges with numerous symposia. As the editor of a recent bilingual edition of Borges's *Selected Poems* (Viking), I was invited to take part in a roundtable on the poetry of Borges. The symposium—which included such distinguished figures as the Argentinian poet Juan Gelman and the Colombian poet and novelist Alvaro Mutis—went off without a hitch, and one could only be impressed by this example of Mexican cultural catholicity. It is not at all clear that Buenos Aires would do as much for a comparable Mexican figure like the late Octavio Paz.

That's the good news about Mexico. My recent visit reminded me that there is plenty of bad news as well. Although I was there for only four days, it was long enough to recognize that Mexico is a country in crisis. If I say this with surprise, it is because nothing in the American press prepared me for the reality of present-day Mexico. The political and financial imperatives flowing from the North American Free Trade Agreement (NAFTA) seem to have tranquillized reporting about Mexico. For example, an upbeat story on the front page of *The Wall Street Journal* recently told readers that "What Southeast was to U.S. Companies, Mexico is Becoming." "In the five years since the passage of the North American Free Trade Agreement," the *Journal* reported, "U.S. manufacturers have moved in flocks south of the border, turning once-sleepy towns into rush-hour cities." But that pleasant prospect is belied by the fact that Mexico is undergoing its most extreme crisis since the revolution seventy-odd years ago.

The truth is that Mexico is struggling with a series of calamities, most of them man-made but a few of meteorological provenance. Each separately is serious; together they threaten to plunge the country into anarchy. It is a measure of the stalwartness of the present president, Ernesto Zedillo, now in his last year of his six-year term, that he is still viewed by most Mexicans with some degree of affection and sympathy.

Let's start with the economy. During Zedillo's term, the buying power of the Mexican worker has declined by 47 percent. Since 1976, the buying power of that same worker has lost 93 percent of its value. Put another way, the same salary in 1999 buys you 7 percent of what you could have bought in 1976. Most Mexican families, except the garish plutocrats, are working at least two jobs. Hunger is evident in both city and country. The hijacking of full grocery carts in supermarket parking lots is not uncommon. In the busy downtown streets on a bright Saturday morning, each block had at least six uniformed policemen strung along the sidewalks.

Violent crime is rampant. Safety from open assault on the streets of Mexico City is clearly a major concern of editorial writers and commentators. At my hotel, when I inquired how I should get to a downtown museum for what turned out to be a superb exhibition of Mayan artifacts, the concierge told me that

> For reasons of safety (*seguridad*), you must rent a limousine arranged by us for approximately three hours. The driver will take you to the entrance to the museum or else accompany you there. Make an appointment with him to be at that same spot after your visit of an hour and a half or so. Do not walk about the streets by yourself.

The budgetary crisis that began in the mid-1980s is ongoing, ameliorated from time to time by bailouts from the U.S. treasury. Barebones national budgets are scheduled for at least the next few years. The International Monetary Fund hovers over all questions of domestic spending. In March 1998, the government finally admitted that it had taken over in 1995 some $62 billion in non-performing loans from about-to-fail banks. This represented 16 percent of the Mexican GNP for that year.

The influence of drug money and culture is also evident everywhere. It has invaded the lowest and highest echelons of the government and has been the subject of extensive coverage in U.S. journals. To take the most notorious of examples from a few years back, President Zedillo had by 1996 despaired of using the infamously corrupt police force to make any headway with the war on drugs. He turned to the Mexican Army, created a National Institute for Combat Against Drugs, and named a ferocious-looking general, Jesús Gutiérrez Rebollo, as its first czar. The White House point man on drugs, General Barry McCaffrey, described General Rebollo as a "soldier of absolute, unquestioned integrity." After a mere two months, Rebollo was found to be living in a luxurious apartment owned by a feared drug dealer and taking bribes. He was cashiered and put on trial. The terrifying formula of the narcotraffickers may explain much: "¿O plomo o plata?," i.e., either accept our lead (in the form of bullets) or our silver (that is, our cash bribes).

Then there is also the matter of the single-party system and the dominance of the PRI, the Institutional Revolutionary Party. The previous president, Carlos Salinas de Gortari, nominated the popular Donaldo Colosio as his successor, but Colosio was assassinated under circumstances that remain murky. Sr. Zedillo, who had no ambitions to be president, was the substitute candidate. The corruption in the previous administration led to the conviction of the former president's brother, Raúl Salinas de Gortari—for conspiracy to murder his ex-brother-in-law Francisco Ruiz Massieu, a rising star in the PRI—and to the discovery of $115 million spread around his 289 bank accounts in the U.S. and Europe. The ex-president himself, Carlos Salinas de Gortari, is in voluntary exile in Dublin, somehow reluctant to return to Mexico. Even President Zedillo is under a cloud; a Mexican banker now in an Australian jail fighting extradition alleges that he gave $4 million in illegal contributions to the 1994 Zedillo campaign. The reporter Tim Golden's conclusions in *The New York Times* (July 11, 1997) about the ubiquity of the bribe in Mexico (known as "la mordida," or "the bite") are more germane than ever:

After insisting for years that Mexican corruption was an old affliction being cured by a new generation of political leaders, senior American officials have begun to acknowledge that the growing power and influence of drug traffickers have led to a law-enforcement crisis so deep that it threatens the stability of a country that shares almost 2000 miles of border with the United States.

And then there is the weather. During the Fall, the coastal and southern parts of Mexico were devastated by torrential rains. The tourist areas of Veracruz, Oaxaca, and Acapulco—tourism is Mexico's second largest industry—were severely affected and the damage to crops has been immense and irreparable. Thousands upon thousands of livelihoods have been ruined, as have the structures, however humble, that many Mexican peasants have been able to call home. In beleaguered communities, still isolated by washed-out roads and bridges, even the bare necessities—potable water, basic nutrition—are lacking. Imprudently, Zedillo has refused all outside help.

I have saved the worst element in this bleak picture for last. There is a strike on in Mexico, one that has paralyzed the country from Zedillo on down. It is a strike of students at UNAM, the National Autonomous University of Mexico. This strike has no parallel in American higher education. The events at Berkeley, Wisconsin, or Columbia in 1968 pale beside the damage already done to Mexico's major institution of higher learning, and there is no amelioration or compromise on the horizon. The facts of the matter are daunting.

The gargantuan university called UNAM is the alma mater of the nation. Located at the southern fringe of Mexico City and occupying a campus which is a city in itself, it is the largest university in Latin America, perhaps in the world. Publicly funded by the federal government with a budget now approaching the peso equivalent of $1 billion a year, it has an enrollment of 270,000 students supported by a staff and faculty of around 30,000. It is governed by a single rector, who in turn is voted in by the fifteen members of a supervisory junta; this group in turn names the directors of programs and research institutes and the chairmen of departments from a list supplied by the rector. But the rector is at the top of this academic pyramid, and it is he who gives intellectual direction and establishes priorities for the future. A special feature of UNAM is its close relation to a chain of public secondary schools; graduates from these schools are eligible for admission to the university without entrance examinations.

In late April, Rector Francisco Barnés proposed drastic reforms. With the aim of raising faculty salaries, upgrading the infrastructure, expanding the library and computer facilities, and boosting scholarship funds, he announced a raise in annual tuition from the present ludicrous equivalent of two American cents to a fee equal to $120. This was to be the first adjustment of fees in some fifty years. He also proposed expelling students who did not finish promptly and terminating the automatic entrance from high school. The poorest students would be exempt from the higher fees, while others slightly better off could postpone payment until they were wage-earners themselves. False data on any scholarship application would result in denial of admission or expulsion. A special feature of Rector Barnés's proposal was that all students currently enrolled were exempt from any future payments. The new tuition fee schedule was to apply to students enrolling in 1999 and thereafter.

The students organized quickly, reacting to what they viewed as the first step toward the "privatization" of a wholly populist educational enterprise. A strike was called, a good number of students joined in, with more than a smattering of disaffected faculty. The university city, with all its satellite buildings, has been occupied and the campus closed since late April. A minority of students was able to struggle on in off-campus buildings and finish with final examinations. At the end of October, the students celebrated the sixth month of the occupation with a festive grand ball accompanied by the inevitable rock band.

It should be said that on June 7 the rector backed down and rescinded the projected fee plan. But by then the movement had taken on a life of its own and a whole series of demands was formulated, having to do with free university education for all, open admission from any high school, and elimination of time-to-degree limitations. One demand even stipulated that governance of the entire university was to be transferred to a board which would judge all educational programs and research in terms of their relevance to "the interests of the Mexican people."

On June 8 a dispatch from Mexico City published in *The New York Times* announced that "the administration [of the university] backed down before

the students' protests, opening the way for a settle-
ment." But as of this writing there is still no set-
tlement, nor is there likely to be one any time soon.
Meanwhile, there have been meetings with student
leaders; committees of concerned emeriti professors
trying to intervene; attempts at "dialogue;" "non-
negotiable" positions announced *urbi et orbi*; mobil-
izations; verbal and at times severely physical
confrontations; takeovers of buildings; failed attempts
at dislodging the squatters; and even a few short-term
kidnappings of strike leaders who have been swept off
their feet into unmarked cars only to be released a few
hours later unharmed.

Comandante Marcos, leader of the Chiapas revolt
in southern Mexico, now celebrating "the 507th anniversary of the indigenous resistance to the
colonizer," says that he approves of the student strike
"because they are right." Masked rebels have visited
the occupied campus, and students have gone south to
Chiapas as a gesture of solidarity.

Although it seems that a moderate majority of students want to see an end to the strike, the ultras on
the left are in control of the situation. They envisage
the demise of the present system as a direct path to a
wholly reorganized system of higher education that is
devoid of corrupting alliances with capitalism in
general, above all of the North American variety with
its reliance on things like computing, economics, ac-
counting, and other sciences. In early November, the
students are upping the ante, violently blocking traffic
in the already clogged city. When the Papal Nuncio,

Monsignor Justo Mullor García, found himself in a five-hour traffic jam engineered by the strikers, he commented: "This is not the way to have a dialogue." Amen.

The more conservative newspapers in the city have been clamoring for police and/or army intervention for months. Even the liberal newspapers, although initially sympathetic to the students, have been discreetly suggesting some kind of action to dislodge the strikers and bring the campus back to normality. President Zedillo has denounced the "brutal aggression" of the students, and noted that "legitimate means can be used by the state to recover the occupied buildings." He appealed to the "silent majority" of students and alumni to take back the university from the miscreants. The rector and 150 professors spoke to the president at the end of August and asked him to intervene, but nothing has happened. One disenchanted professor said that asking the president to intervene was as efficacious as writing a letter to Santa Claus. So the question remains—is there no way to intervene in this educational and social catastrophe?

One problem is that there is no such thing as short-term memory in Mexico. Everyone remembers the army interventions just prior to the opening of the Olympics in Mexico City in 1968. President Gustavo Díaz Ordaz was increasingly irritated by student protests against the extravagant expenses incurred during the months prior to the opening, and he finally warned the students that new protests would be stopped "to avoid any further loss of prestige." According to Alan Riding in his excellent *Distant Neighbors: A Portrait of the Mexicans* (1984), there was yet another meeting which took place in Tlatelolco Square in early October 1968, a meeting which ended with the army raking the whole square with machine-gun fire. The estimates of the dead range from two to three hundred, though friends tell me that a thousand is not out of the question. In any case, the blood was washed away by firetrucks that same evening, and the Olympics started on time. President Zedillo, of the same, now-weakened, party as Díaz Ordaz, is reluctant to have his government make another move against student protestors. Inevitably, students and soldiers or police will die in such a confrontation. The students know that the government has been defanged by the events of 1968. When the army has been sent out to clear students from the highways in recent days, the young soldiers from the provinces are without pistols, rifles, or even the equivalent of nightsticks. They are issued only plastic shields to protect themselves against the torrent of rocks sent their way. The soldiers then throw the rocks back in the direction of the squatters.

With an election scheduled for July 2000, Zedillo does not want to be seen to jeopardize his party's chances by intervening vigorously in the strike. In a poll of four hundred citizens taken by the newspaper *El Universal*, 55 percent said that the government should intervene, 45 percent said that it should not. In all, 31 percent said that the fault lay with the intransigence of the rector, 25 percent blamed Zedillo, 11 percent said the students were at fault.

Although most of those polled thought that classes at UNAM would begin again sometime this year, time is running out. My friends opined that Zedillo will dump the problem onto the lap of his successor, which means that UNAM will not open till Fall 2000, if then. The push and pull between ultras and moderates is an ongoing thing. Many of the most fervid participants are students in the UNAM-related secondary schools. Speaking to a journalist, one striker noted that "they called us Generation X, but we are showing them that we are a fighting generation not seen since '68." On the other hand, the faculty of the Schools of Veterinary Medicine, Social Work, and Political Science announced in late October that the student movement of 1999 "had lost its direction, is without consensus or rationality; they are people who believe that the university is only a trench from which ideological class struggles are launched."

The renowned liberal commentator Carlos Monsivais reluctantly had to admit that

> I do not deny the immense responsibility carried by the university authorities for the shutdown of the university, but I must take note of the enormous degree of irritation the demonstrations have caused, the extremism without political or ideological validation, the deluge of Che Guevara and Mao portraits devoid of historical context, the level of intransigence demonstrated by the strikers.

Nine research institutes have been taken over, one the Geology Institute which warns the public about possible seismic activity. The staff of this institute was thrown out of its quarters forcibly. Their supervisor had a few things to say to the "students." "I am leaving behind eighty projects and delicate equipment worth two-and-a-half-million dollars. I hope you know what to do with it."

Student sentinels are now posted at all entrances to the campus, searching all visitors. If anyone protests at these procedures, the response is, "The people demand it! The university is paid for by the people! That's why it is yours! Defend it!" A sinister breach between polarized groups in confrontation grows wider every day. The situation gives ominous new relevance to the American phrase "Mexican stand-off."

December 1999

Letter from Vienna

I MPORTANT CHANGES are evident in Vienna these days. When I was there in March, for the first time in my memory, there was a real sense of political turmoil, occasioned by the recent entry into Chancellor Wolfgang Schüssel's government of the right-wing Freedom Party, and its putative leader, Mr. Jörg Haider. For the past fifty years, the government, with its chancellors changing every few years, has been made up of an ongoing cozy coalition between the two major parties dominant in the postwar period—the Social Democratic Party (SPOE, known colloquially as "the Reds,") and the Austria People's Party (OEVP, "the Blacks"). Haider and his party have put an end to all that. People are uneasy.

On the surface, things did not seem to have changed in any drastic fashion. The city itself, which counts on its easygoing ways and ample dispensing of *gemütlichkeit* for tourists, does seem to be surreptitiously taking on something of the aluminum-and-glass air of a German city, accompanied by a pretense to efficiency decidedly un-Austrian. Some of the cafés have turned into automobile showrooms or computer salons. The cafés that remain do still contribute to the atmospheric attraction much touted by the ministry of tourism in its brochures. Indeed, the admirable and most definitely unspoken rule of letting all customers remain at their respective tables for as long as they like is still inviolate.

I visited two remarkable museums. The "Collection of Ancient Musical Instruments" in the Hofburg Palace has an ingenious audio feature. As you approach with earphones one of the glass cases containing a particular set of old instruments, what seems to be a short-distance FM broadcast of these same instruments being expertly played fills the ear. As you move on and approach another family of instruments, be they a consort of viols, sackbuts, klappentrumpets, serpents or waldhorns, the music just heard fades away and the instruments you are now approaching begin to sound. In this way, the viewer/listener has the freedom to move back, forth, and around, and is not condemned to a one-way tour imposed by a cassette tape.

The Jewish Museum of the City of Vienna, on the Dorotheergasse, just down from the auction house called the Dorotheum (where the flotsam of old Vienna is on view in all its kitschy glory), is a moving documentation of the fate of Jewry in Vienna over the centuries, from the founding of the first ghetto in the thirteenth century through assimilation in the nineteenth and early twentieth, and on to the 1938 *Kristallnacht* and the subsequent genocidal deportations and the razing of the principal temples in Vienna.

The city must be the most compact and accessible

tourist site in Europe. As is well known to any reader of Carl Schorske's *Fin-de-Siècle Vienna: Politics and Culture*, the Emperor Franz Josef ordered the ring of fortress walls torn down in 1857 and a grand series of monumental buildings constructed in their place, resulting in what is now the opera, the parliament, the city hall, the university, the Kunsthistorisches Museum, etc. As Schorske pointed out, the monumentality of these edifices was clearly designed to belittle the spectator/citizen and magnify the glory of crown and empire. But the point is, the old fortress walls held the city in for so long, that the result was an extraordinarily compact and concentrated center of town. The tram (#1) circling the Ring now takes some twenty-five minutes to complete one circumferential tour. From my hotel on the Park Ring just across from the gilded Johann Strauss memorial in the Stadtpark, the Opera is a twelve-minute walk, the Musikverein (home of the Vienna Philharmonic) a mere ten minutes, the Konzerthaus (with two chamber halls and a large orchestral hall) eight minutes. Though I was certainly not looking for one, I did not happen upon a single movie house within the center of the city.

As one would expect, the abundance of musical performances was extraordinary, though, perhaps out of happenstance, visiting artists dominated the scene—Murray Perahia's recital featuring a very un-Gouldian performance of the "Goldberg Variations," heavily-pedaled and almost romantic, a stunning concert of Bartok and Beethoven quartets by the Vermeer Quartet, a wild and woolly performance by Sir Simon

Rattle and the City of Birmingham Symphony Orchestra of works by György Ligeti and Olivier Messiaen. The intensity of silence amidst an audience in Vienna during musical performances is a phenomenon not to be duplicated anywhere else, certainly not New York. Again, maybe it was just chance, but it was difficult to erase the memory of past performances heard in these same halls—Klemperer's unforgettable *German Requiem* of Brahms (the conductor half-paralyzed from a stroke and looking for all the world like Mozart's "stone guest"), von Karajan directing the B Minor Mass of Bach, and his haunting concert of Palestrina masses at ten A.M. at the Opera House one Sunday morning in the early Sixties.

At the same Vienna State Opera, it was heartening and reassuring to see and hear Alban Berg's *Wozzeck* done with such blistering intensity. The leading role was sung by Franz Grundheber, who has already set down his reading of the role in the splendid recording directed by Claudio Abbado. The role of Marie was passionately sung—close to hysteria—with a sultry stage presence by Deborah Polaski in her Vienna debut. A few evenings later, I saw an equally intense *Otello* featuring Kristjan Johansson as Otello, of whom much more will be heard, and the veteran Renato Bruson as Iago. A singer I had not heard before, Adrianna Pieczonka, was a superb Desdemona. It is good to be reminded that the splendid orchestral playing at the Vienna State Opera is due above all to the fact that the Vienna Philharmonic is the pit orchestra for every performance. The subtlety of sound and the way they listen to each other explain in good measure why the musical results are always so distinguished, night after night.

In the end, the spectacle of Vienna and its not-so-distant past is daunting, even overwhelming. It is a repeatedly observed irony that the city that drove out Freud and most certainly hounded out Arnold Schoenberg is the same city that now celebrates these two seminal figures with splendid memorial museums. Gustav Mahler said it all less than a century ago with an anguished rhetorical question: "Do you really have to be dead in Austria before they'll let you live?"

In my previous visits, I hadn't taken in the Freud Museum at Berggasse 19, and it is impossible to do justice in a few words to the scrupulous care for iconographic detail that the Freud apartment now offers to the inquiring observer. More revealing from my point of view as a music lover was the recently opened Arnold Schoenberg Center, not described in even the most recent guide books I have consulted. It is located at the lower part of the grand Schwarzenberg Platz, Zaunergasse 1-3, just to the left of the monstrous memorial to the Russian Army erected during the Soviet occupation. (This dreadful thing is thankfully not illuminated at night and, moreover, is obscured by a seventy-foot jet spray which ever so artfully makes it disappear). The Schoenberg Center displays a detailed re-creation of Schoenberg's working office transported from his home in Los Angeles, and a complete library of Schoenbergiana, including a representative selection of his paintings. A particular matter of interest is the detailed scrutiny of the Kandinsky/Schoenberg relationship contained in a special exhibition—not only a rich selection of Kandinsky's paintings, but also a magnificent sampling of work done by his contemporaneous Russian colleagues that up to now had lain forgotten in the cellars of the Russian Museum in Saint Petersburg. An informative slide show with narration, showing key declarations from the Kandinsky/Schoenberg correspondence, demonstrates how both artists saw in each other a symbiosis of interests, glimpsing the music and the painting of the future.

I was fortunate to be invited to an informal supper in the apartment of the Argentine novelist Victoria Slavuski, whose name I knew from her discerning article on Borges, "The Old Man and the City," published in the *Times Literary Supplement* last August. A crash course in Austrian politics ensued until the wee hours, and of course the name of Jörg Haider was never far from the preoccupations of this friendly group of United Nations employees, journalists, and one member of the Austrian foreign ministry. I was reminded that Austria now has the highest percentage of aliens of any country in the European Union, and that the coalition between "Reds" and "Blacks" had unravelled in the last election, giving Haider's party 27 percent of the vote, when he had started a decade or so ago with only a fringe of 4 percent at most.

A common theme throughout the evening was the fact that, although xenophobia, anti-Socialist stances, and veiled Nazi sympathies were characteristic of

Haider in some of his most virulent public declarations, the voters who had split off from the other two parties had little interest in his ideology, though this seems to be the sole point of interest on the part of American and other European observers. Rather, Haider represents the essence of the politically incorrect in Austria today; he is a sworn enemy of the "Proporz" system established just after the war, whereby "Reds" and "Blacks" controlled practically all state jobs in Austria—post office, ministries, education, medicine, etc. Without a party card, there was no employment, just as in the Iron Curtain countries. Something of a sinister yuppie, Haider is a computer and physical fitness fanatic garbed in designer jeans who drives a sleek Porsche—a veritable bull in the Austrian porcelain shop. Always to be kept in mind is the fact that he is still governor of Carinthia, well-known as the most chauvinist and nationalistic of provinces, nestled on the border with Slovenia and the first reception center for refugees from the dismemberment of the former Yugoslavia. Moreover, he has learned quickly from certain pages of contemporary American political history. Indeed, his "Contract with Austria" asks for frugality, reduction in taxes, more incentives for business, an end to early retirement, elimination of the national debt, defense of national sovereignty in relation to the bureaucrats in Brussels and the European Union as a whole, restrictions on immigration, deregulation, and privatization, and market reforms to encourage entrepreneurship—quite necessary considering that the Austrian state still owns the telephone company and the main tobacco corporation.

In early February, the European Union imposed sanctions on the government headed by Chancellor Schüssel solely on the grounds of his dalliance with the Freedom Party. These sanctions entail suspension of normal diplomatic communication, pro forma reception of its diplomats, and no support on behalf of Austrian candidates for international appointments. It is not clear on what legal basis the EU has proceeded in the way that it has. The BBC man in Vienna, Angus Roxburgh, noted that "the EU is on thin ice in imposing sanctions on the fear of future violations rather than because of any infractions in the new government's programme." There have been no violations, everyone is on his best behavior. The whole process has been a model of democratic elections and the usual deal-making. Furthermore, there is no "let-out" clause in the sanctions that defines what Austria must do in order to bring the sanctions to an end. My conversants that evening were sorely divided on the matter of the EU move. On the one hand, a minority felt that since all procedures were above board and the elections absolutely untainted, a preventive sanction such as this, treating Austria like a "Teheran" or "Milosević," will in the end produce an adverse reaction in the country, and give more power and martyrdom to Haider and his party. On the other hand, most in the room felt that the move by the EU was a needed blunderbuss shot across the bow of Schüssel's ship of state, and aimed also at any other European country or leader that might be contemplating a serious collaboration with the extreme right. In that sense, it was welcome. But there is a feeling of quiet alarm and a deep sense of foreboding.

Some amelioration may be found in attitudes and actions of a few wild cards within the Freedom Party, though under Haider's brusque and authoritarian dominance, they are increasingly rare. The candidate for the powerful finance post put forth by the party, but not Haider's choice, is the now approved Karl-Heinz Grasser, thirty-one years old, a cool free-marketer with rimless glasses and natty cravats, a character eons away from the thuggish populism of Haider. Just recently, Haider resigned as head of his party, but this move is seen as a ploy to remove the party from the barrage of attacks that he and his closest associates have brought down upon it. The general feeling is that he is still pulling all the strings from his redoubt in Klagenfurt, Carinthia.

It is not lost on any observer that Haider himself is resolutely anti-intellectual, and a vituperative opponent, for instance, of the Burgtheater producing one of the late Thomas Bernhard's last plays, an excoriation of Austria entitled *Heldenplatz*. He is against governmental subsidies of the arts in principle. Obviously there are cultural implications here—the director of the heavily subsidized Salzburg Festival, Gérard Mortier, had handed in his resignation, but just lately retracted it in paradoxical protest against the government's alliance with the Freedom Party. He says that he is henceforth going to carry out a cultural offensive in Salzburg for the remainder of his contract. The dramatist Elfriede Jelinek, object of more than a few tirades from Haider,[*] has now declared that under no circumstances can her work be presented in Austria until the coalition with Haider and his party has been dissolved. I arrived just one month too late to attend the anti-Haider demonstration on February 19th in the Heldenplatz, the same locale where Hitler had harangued the crowds after the Anschluss some sixty-two years ago. A highly motivated throng of 300,000 Austrians gathered against the coalition with Haider.

Something of a paralysis or a standoff now is in place. The EU, during its so-called "dot.com" summit in Lisbon, tried to keep Chancellor Schüssel from the customary group photo taken after the deliberations. According to the *International Herald Tribune*, the Portuguese prime minister "found a diplomatic way out by organizing a group photograph with President Ernesto Zedillo of Mexico, who attended the summit to sign a free-trade agreement with the EU." In this photograph, Schüssel is seen standing next to Tony Blair, who in turn seems engaged in a scrutiny of the clouds, his head resolutely turned away from the Austrian. Such antics are bound to continue.

A Vienna friend told me of a graffito recently seen: "Knowledge pursues me, but I am faster." Haider is fast on his feet also. The only question for Austria is, will knowledge ever catch up to him?

May 2000

---

* [Not, I feel sure John would agree, *undeserved* tirades.—*Ed.*]